Bill Hull and Brandon Cook point to Dietrich Bonhoeffer's path, which is the journey away from cheap grace and toward costly discipleship. This is an important book for serious Christians to work through. It grapples with the fundamental issue of what it really means to place our faith in Christ and follow him. I recommend the content of this book for serious reflection.

BOBBY HARRINGTON, founder and director of Discipleship.org and Renew.org

The Cost of Cheap Grace is refreshing for those who long to learn about Jesus' life and teaching about discipleship (which is so rarely reaffirmed) and rebuking for those who have wandered into a self-defined, alternate version of discipleship. Bill Hull and Brandon Cook clearly remind us of the calling Jesus set before us and help us juxtapose it against contemporary teaching that has invaded our theology and churches. I anticipate that after our dozens of house-church pastors and network of churches in the Church Project read *The Cost of Cheap Grace*, our decisions to deny ourselves, take up our cross, and follow Jesus will radically increase.

JASON SHEPPERD, lead pastor of Church Project

Briskly written, theologically rich, and always engaging, *The Cost of Cheap Grace* uncovers the roots of the nominalism that undermines the church's witness to the world. Brandon and Bill offer biblical, practical, and challenging pathways to transform your disciple making. This enjoyable book will supercharge you and your church!

ALEX ABSALOM, founder of Dandelion Resourcing, coauthor of *Discipleship That Fits*

The popular understanding of grace has been a costly deception, causing many to buy a cheap imitation of God's original. Hull and Cook joyfully invite us into grace's ability to fully transform us through true discipleship. This is a potent read for every follower of Jesus who longs for a life of ever-deepening union with God.

DR. LARRY J. WALKEMEYER, lead pastor of Light & Life Christian Fellowship

Like a clap of lightning splitting the darkness or the sound of a muffled drone, *The Cost of Cheap Grace* is a jolt to a nation of us struggling to focus on the singular work of discipleship. Bill Hull and Brandon Cook begin upstream at the source, where we're encouraged to rethink our conception of Jesus' gospel so we might better imagine the makeup of a disciple of Jesus. After guiding us through a litany of factors contributing to our lethargy toward discipleship—cultural and theological, historical and philosophical—they put us on the line. Will we stand up and start walking?

KYU HO LEE, Navigators 20s leader in Los Angeles/Orange County, CA

Bill and Brandon challenge the theology and church culture that have created a chasm among followers of Jesus. They aren't, however, simply doom-and-gloom prophets, but rather they point us toward a better way forward with thoughtful insights and practical advice. The introduction alone is worth the price of the book and will make you yearn for a better way forward for the church.

MIKE GOLDSWORTHY, pastor, author, and adjunct professor

This book was refreshing, life-giving, freeing, and deeply meaningful to my walk with God and to my pastorate. I was encouraged and challenged, and I received great hope to step into the responsibility of sounding the clarion call: Following Jesus begins and ends with grace, but the middle is filled with a path paved by our willingness to obey Jesus' words and emulate his life through the power of the Holy Spirit.

KELLY M. WILLIAMS, senior pastor of Vanguard Church

THE COST OF CHEAP GRACE

A NavPress resource published in alliance
with Tyndale House Publishers, Inc.

THE COST OF CHEAP GRACE

BILL HULL & BRANDON COOK

RECLAIMING THE VALUE OF DISCIPLESHIP

NavPress is the publishing ministry of The Navigators, an international Christian organization and leader in personal spiritual development. NavPress is committed to helping people grow spiritually and enjoy lives of meaning and hope through personal and group resources that are biblically rooted, culturally relevant, and highly practical.

For more information, visit www.NavPress.com.

IN MEMORIAM

BILL

We remember Eugene Peterson as we publish this work. His impact on both of us has been immense.

I have been reading him for years and have always been awestruck by his capacity with words. His very life as a pastor was both a rebuke and a lifeline. I recall him telling a story about going to a very hip conference, a leading-edge environment. He said that the experience sucked all the Jesus out of him. It took him a week of reading Karl Barth's Church Dogmatics *to set him right. He said that things were so different, it was like he was seeing the world through a unique set of eyes. He recommended dedicating seminary education's first year to reading great novels and literature. This had to do with expanding the pastoral imagination. I recently saw a short film on his life. When the interviewer asked him what he hoped the effect of his life had been, he said he hoped he was able to change American pastors' imaginations. I know he did mine—he got me to slow down, think, and pray.*

In that tradition, Brandon and I hope to get you, the reader, to expand your understanding of what it means to be saved. In the end, we hope that you agree with us that salvation without discipleship is not salvation at all but a cheap imitation of what God offers us. We may need to live outside our safe mental boxes, to leave our either/or world and live in the both/and world. Eugene Peterson was an expert at expanding our understanding and helping us embrace paradox. So here's to you, Eugene: Well done.

The fundamental hallmark of belief is how you act.

WISDOM OF THE AGES

Faith is only real when there is obedience.

DIETRICH BONHOEFFER

I think we ought to read only the kind of books that wound or stab us. If the book we are reading doesn't wake us up with a blow to the head, what are we reading it for?

FRANZ KAFKA

CONTENTS

BILL

"SALVATION BY GRACE ALONE." It's a modern theological cliché—by definition, "a phrase or opinion that is overused and betrays a lack of original thought."[1] This cliché has become the way you establish your bona fide evangelical credentials. It is meant to bolster a doctrine that emerged from the Reformation, that salvation has nothing to do with behavior. The phrase has provided a secure hiding place for millions, somewhere they could rest from the obvious labor the gospel requires. The divorcing of grace from behavior is responsible for the church relieving itself of the moral burden to live better and be better than the general population. Dietrich Bonhoeffer applied his stinging rebuke of this development in his 1937 manual for ministers, *The Cost of Discipleship*.

> Cheap grace means justification of sin but not of the sinner. . . .
> The church that teaches this doctrine of grace thereby confers such grace upon itself. The world finds in this church a cheap cover-up for its sins.[2]

There are actually Christians who proudly proclaim that they are no better behaved than people of other religions or no religions at all. If this is the gospel—that you are saved, you get your sins forgiven, and you gain entrance into heaven but that your morality, behavior, and the collective contribution of the church will not improve life on earth—why would anyone be interested? Any honest person with moral integrity would be repulsed by such an idea. Skeptics would (rightly) say, "Christians go to heaven regardless of life and conduct, but non-Christians go to hell forever, even if they live better and contribute more to society." Even flawed humans reserve life sentences for only the most heinous crimes.

So we can conclude that "salvation by grace alone" is a cliché: It clearly reveals a lack of thought. But it's a cliché with consequence: What it has created is cleverly presented in the classic novel *The Brothers Karamazov.*

THE GRAND INQUISITOR

One of Fyodor Dostoevsky's famous brothers, Ivan, keeps a notebook of God's mistakes—particularly atrocities that God has allowed. Dostoevsky uses newspaper headlines similar to real events recorded in 1876 to make Ivan's argument: [3]

- the nobleman who orders his hounds to tear a peasant boy to pieces in front of his mother
- the man who beats his struggling horse
- the parents who lock their tiny daughter in a freezing privy all night while she knocks on the walls, pleading for mercy

- the Turk who entertains a baby with a shiny pistol before blowing its brains out[4]

Alyosha, Ivan's brother, believes in God and his goodness but cannot counter Ivan's argument, which culminates in the story of the Grand Inquisitor, Ivan's indictment of the hypocritical church.

The story Ivan tells takes place in Seville in the 1500s, during the period of the Inquisition. Jesus has come to Seville and moves about silently, but he is recognized immediately. People are drawn to him—they follow him; they gather around him. He stretches out his arms to the people, and just by touching them, his healing power begins to flow. The blind can see, the lame walk, and people weep and kiss the ground where he has walked. He stops at the cathedral steps, where a small white coffin sits with a dead little girl inside. The mother throws herself at his feet, Jesus reaches out, and the girl rises from the dead. There is shouting and weeping.

Just then the Cardinal of Seville, the Grand Inquisitor, crosses the cathedral square. He notices what has happened, recognizes Jesus, and promptly has him arrested.

The Grand Inquisitor comes to Jesus' dark cell, holding a light. He doesn't speak for two minutes, and then he lays the light down.

"You? Is it really you?"

Jesus has come at a very bad time, the Inquisitor proclaims. He is making things difficult for the church leaders, interfering with their business. "The church is no longer yours to run," he tells Jesus; his authority has been transferred to the pope. "It has taken us fifteen hundred years to reduce the burdensome and unrealistic demands you left behind. We can't have you coming back and undoing all that good work, dogma, and traditions of the church. Tomorrow, I will pronounce you a heretic, and the people will believe me."

Jesus never speaks a word. He only walks over to the old man and kisses him gently on his old, bloodless lips. The old man quivers, walks to the door, and says, "Go now, and do not come back . . . ever. You must never, never come again!" And he lets the prisoner out into the dark streets of the city.[5]

The Grand Inquisitor understands (and our contemporary church unconsciously recognizes) that Jesus comes with a gospel that expects personal change—and not just in general temperament or by ceasing to commit socially unacceptable sins. The Jesus who lives among us demands everything of us. Another word for that is *discipleship*.

The discipleship that Jesus offers us as his gospel is a matter of *following him and learning from him how to live our lives as though he were living them.*[6] That alone constitutes a saved life; everything else is a cheap imitation.

It's the cheap imitation that the Grand Inquisitor insists the church had worked hard to create and didn't want to give up. When Jesus shows up, even if only briefly, this cheap imitation of the gospel begins to crumble: Everyone knows it is him, and lives are changed immediately in ways that the imitation can't imitate. Many present-day "Christians" have no serious expectation that Jesus will return as he promised—which is a good thing for their psyches, because if he did, most of them would not like what came with him, much less want to spend eternity in his presence. In the eyes of the modern world, the Jesus of the Bible is intolerant, judgmental, harsh, and unforgiving toward the unrepentant.

THE THREAT OF DISCIPLESHIP

The only man who has the right to say that he is justified by grace alone is the man who has left all to follow Christ. Such a man knows that the call to discipleship is a gift of grace, and that the call is inseparable from the grace.

DIETRICH BONHOEFFER, *THE COST OF DISCIPLESHIP*

Dietrich Bonhoeffer makes this assertion as a way of reconciling two seemingly incompatible ideas, at least according to the spirit of the age: grace and discipleship. It is the person who has given the most to his or her salvation, Bonhoeffer recognizes, who understands best that only by grace could they have lived it out. Here Bonhoeffer echoes a powerful call from the apostle Paul: "Work hard to show the results of your salvation, obeying God with deep reverence and fear" (Philippians 2:12, NLT). The more you place yourself at risk, the more profound are your experiences of grace and mercy—you come to know, at a bone-deep level, that it is all by grace. This is a knowledge that is never gained by semiobedient people or by the majority of Christians.

Bonhoeffer was significantly influenced by Martin Luther. He agreed with Luther's emphasis on "justification by faith alone" (a companion assertion to the clichéd "salvation by grace alone") and defended it. In fact, Bonhoeffer lamented the damage that had been done to Luther's teaching:

Nonetheless, what emerged victorious from Reformation history was not Luther's recognition of pure, costly grace, but the alert religious instinct of human beings for the place where grace could be had the cheapest. Only a small, hardly noticeable distortion of the emphasis was needed, and that most dangerous and ruinous deed was done. . . . Luther knew that this grace had cost him one life and daily continued to cost him, for he was not excused by grace from discipleship, but instead was all the more thrust into it.

Bonhoeffer went on to connect the "ruinous deed" to people's lives.

The followers' own teaching ["by grace alone"] was, therefore, unassailable, judged by Luther's teaching, but their teaching meant the end and the destruction of the Reformation as the revelation of God's costly grace on earth. The justification of the sinner in the world became the justification of sin and the world. Without discipleship, costly grace would become cheap grace.[7]

This ruinous deed led to the favorite evangelical bumper sticker of the 1980s, "Christians aren't perfect, just forgiven." In other words, don't expect much from us.

The "ruinous deed" Luther's followers committed was done primarily because they were human and did what humans naturally do: take the easiest, least costly path, which was to separate grace from behavior and responsibility—to separate discipleship to Christ from salvation in Christ, thus making discipleship an optional activity, the optional domain of "serious" Christians. Of course, this led to the creation of a church dominated by nominalism, people who used the church as a community service for birth, marriage, baptism, and death. It is quite common to engage well-meaning people in conversation who present themselves as respectable, nonpracticing Christians who are church members. This, we would venture to say, is the largest Christian demographic on earth.

"Salvation by grace alone" protects the option to live as a partial Christian—to take advantage of religious goods and services, the assurance of heaven, the immediate and unconditional availability of forgiveness. You can come and go as you please, live a selfish life, be critical of the church and its leadership but not help solve the problem—and still get Communion.

This problem is the church's worst-kept secret. Consider the words of Friedrich Nietzsche well over one hundred years ago:

> The Christians have never practiced the actions Jesus
> prescribed to them; and the impudent garrulous talk
> about the "justification by faith" and its supreme
> and sole significance is only the consequence of the
> Church's lack of courage and will to profess the *works*
> Jesus demanded.[8]

We would not sign off on the outworking of Nietzsche's philosophy nor on his ethics, but his critique of the church as he knew it still resonates today. What is sorely needed in our midst is a return to the imitation of Christ in which Jesus' followers demand of themselves and the church Jesus' work in the world and in their own lives.

THE WORLD OF HALF-TRUTH

Like most clichés, "salvation by grace alone" isn't wrong. Complicated ideas are often distilled into shorthand phrases to make them easier to access. Over time, however, such shorthand phrases can come to mean something much different from what their authors meant when they crafted them. The following is what we consider the contemporary understanding of "salvation by grace alone."

Salvation. A person is saved from their sins. Their sins are forgiven, and as a result, they gain admission to heaven. Salvation is thus a singular event focused exclusively on forgiveness of sin, partitioned off from any requirement for behavioral change.

By grace. Grace is a derivative of God's mercy, and the greatest portion of it comes to us at our "point of salvation." This often is called the moment you were "saved" or received new life, forgiveness, new birth—the big moment when you became a child of God. Grace is something you cannot seek or earn; you only receive it. The human's relationship to grace is a passive one: God is the one who distributes it as he wills.

Alone. Alone contrasts grace with human effort. Life in Christ is separate from human action: There is nothing you can do to earn it, there is nothing you can do to lose it, and there is nothing you can do to supplement it.

There is something powerful and right about each of these elements. They are profoundly true: All people need to be saved, salvation can only come about by God's grace, and we are completely unable to achieve salvation on our own. Hardly anyone consciously teaches cheap grace. (Some do, but they are in the minority.) You just don't hear leaders, pastors, or evangelists proudly spouting, "I make everyone who has said the magic sinner's prayer as comfortable as possible in my ministry because I want all their friends to feel welcome. We want all of them to pray the prayer and be baptized. If we remove many of the traditional barriers, we can fill up heaven and our churches. It doesn't really matter how well-behaved or transformed they are here in this life; it is the next life that counts, where everyone will be perfect."

And yet "salvation by grace alone" has a larger meaning, one that cheap grace suppresses. Here is the other side of each word:

SALVATION

Salvation is a comprehensive idea covering the process of God calling a person to a reconciling relationship, leading to repentance, forgiveness, new birth, and a life of following and learning from Jesus. This includes participating in his values and his mission. The culmination of this good life is stepping into the eternal state of an active life with him.

The focus of salvation is much grander than the minimal requirements for making it into heaven. There seem to be endless conversations about Aunt Harriet or Grandpa Joe who made a profession of faith but never lived it out—did they make it? Reading the Gospels, one gets the strong impression that Jesus taught the nature of salvation as more intricate: Salvation to Jesus included individuals, but individuals were not the only focus. God made promises to people and to *his people*. Also, to Jesus, salvation seemed to be more of a process and less of an event. We have made it an event so we can count it and assure people they have nothing to worry about.[9] We will unpack this further over the course of the book.

The spacecraft *Voyager 1* has returned photographs from

what is called interstellar space. One such photo showed a thin vertical shaft of yellow light, inside of which was a white speck. That speck was Earth. The sight of us as that small speck in the vast universe was at the same time frightening and wondrous. The fullness of the gospel has a similar impact. Trying to connect the ancient story of the creator God, the incarnate Word, and the Spirit's vastness and mystery is too much for the human mind. When we think of what God is saving when we say *salvation*, we must remember that it is a much larger project than forgiveness of a single person's sin. The book of Revelation states it in one of its salvation songs:

> Hallelujah! The Salvation, the Glory, the Power all belong to our God. The judgments are accurate and right. He judged the Great Whore! The earth ruined with her cheating sex, and God's servants' blood spilled by her hand He restored to rightness.
> REVELATION 19:1-3, AUTHOR'S PARAPHRASE

Eugene Peterson describes salvation as "the answer to catastrophe"—the totality of the impact of sin on creation:

> All parts of creation—Arcturus and the Mississippi, Lebanon cedars and English turnips, rainbow trout and parula warblers, eskimos and aborigines—have been jarred out of the harmonious original and are in discord. The transparent complementarity of male and female is darkened into rivalry and accusation. The cool evening conversation between God and humans

is distorted into furtive evasions. The "fit" between
heaven and earth, between creation and creature
and Creator, is dislocated: form no longer matches
function, result no longer flows from purpose. Instead
there is pain, travail, sweat, death.

Nothing is exempt from the catastrophe.[10]

Fully appreciating what God goes through, what we all go
through to rescue our planet from the catastrophe could require
a shot of Maalox. Peterson sums up the catastrophe with the
help of novelist Walker Percy's little book *Lost in the Cosmos*: "We
don't know where we are. We don't know who we are."[11]

The simple prayer of a person at an altar or over coffee with
a friend touches this wondrous salvation project but in no way
grasps its massive impact. Salvation is the plot of history; it is
a rescue mission. Salvation is God's action, his project, and it
includes the entire creation.

The world's alternative is to put the world right by good
deeds and so to leave God out. To the secular mind, for God
to conduct himself in the way he sees fit, even though great
human minds cannot fathom it or agree with it, is scandalous.
Many think of God as a megalomaniac because he violates their
modern sensibilities (Isaiah 55:8-9; 1 Corinthians 1:18-25).
But what it takes to turn around the world, save it, and rescue
its people is a strong stomach and an absolute commitment.
Salvation requires bloodshed. Can we agree then not to trivialize
salvation by reducing it to whether a person is safe and secure in
the arms of Christ based on a prayer or religious ritual prescribed
by the priestly class?

BY DISCIPLESHIP

If we replace the word *grace* in "salvation by grace alone" with *discipleship*, we have an entirely different discussion. A disciple is a person who has chosen to position themselves as Jesus' student or follower. Discipleship is a state of being created by the work of the Holy Spirit combined mysteriously with the human will.

Critics object to an emphasis on discipleship because it often functions as shorthand for an individual's personal growth into Christlikeness. They worry about an inbred understanding of Christian maturity that functions at odds with the great commission. They prefer to emphasize "disciple making" over discipleship. We will set aside the question of whether you can be truly Christlike and not make disciples. But it's highly doubtful that any significant movement of God has been inhibited by referring to discipleship rather than disciple making. Reasons for the great commission being diminished in the contemporary Christian imagination run much deeper than word choice. You can't find a church that honors Christ's words that would not agree that making disciples of all nations is crucial. They have had the language right, but they have used the right language wrongly. The church of cheap grace makes disciples, but the disciples they make are by and large practicing a watered-down, broadened-out discipleship, such that just about anything a church does hits the target.

Making new disciples is the starting point for multiplication and the fulfillment of Christ's mandate to reach the world. In Matthew 28:18-20, the centerpiece of the great commission is the command to "make disciples." The critics are right both about the priority given by Jesus to disciple making in his gospel, and about the failures of the contemporary church in making disciples. For our discussion, however, making disciples is inherent to discipleship: It is part of our ongoing interaction with Christ, learning from him and participating in his mission.

When we use the phrase "salvation by discipleship alone," we mean that *there is only one way to fully experience your salvation*, and that is via *a lifetime of discipleship to Christ*. Everyone who is called to salvation is called to discipleship—no exceptions, no excuses.

The reason this book is being written is not to fixate on whether a person who doesn't engage in discipleship is "saved" or not. The question itself reveals how miniaturized our understanding of salvation has become. Many cheap-grace Christians don't even understand what they've been called to because no one has ever shown them what it is or trained them. Our point remains: Discipleship is a normal part of what it means to be saved.

ALONE

Decades ago, it was popular to quote John 14:6: "Jesus told him, 'I am the way, the truth, and the life. No one can come to the Father except through me'" (NLT). Hardly anyone mentions it now. Jesus sounds so antiquated, out of step with the cultural mood here. His assertion seems to represent narrow-mindedness, intolerance, and absolutism. Most such objections to singular truth are self-refuting, however. Lesslie Newbigin speaks of a friend's encounter with a fellow passenger on a flight. "At the end of the conversation, the other man said, 'Well, of one thing I am certain: There is no such thing as absolute truth.' My friend said, 'Are you absolutely sure?'"[12]

Of course, this is logically absurd, even laughable. People are absolutely scandalized by Jesus' absolutist claims. Dallas Willard answered this philosophical scandal: "If Jesus knew a better way, he would be the first to tell you. And if you don't believe that, you don't know much about Jesus."[13]

ONLY ONE WAY TO BECOME JESUS' DISCIPLE

Jesus taught that the only way any person can be his disciple is to follow him. Only those who believe in Jesus follow Jesus. The only way a Christian can know they are a Christian is to follow Jesus. If you wake up one day and find yourself not following Jesus, you must take stock. If you are okay with it, then it's not in your soul. A Christian and a disciple are the same person. To believe Jesus is to trust Jesus is to follow Jesus. When someone follows Jesus, they learn from him and participate in his mission on earth. This is one seamless process, and it is called salvation.

Jesus said it plainly in Luke's Gospel.

If any of you wants to be my follower, you must give up
your own way, take up your cross daily, and follow me.
If you try to hang on to your life, you will lose it. But if
you give up your life for my sake, you will save it.
LUKE 9:23-25, NLT

The Jesus way is not only a message for those considering Christ as the answer to the human crisis. It is an explanation of what he is calling every person to do. It is not ambiguous; it requires a faith that gets your legs moving, your mind and heart engaged in learning and obeying. The way of Christ is the way of the disciple (Luke 14:27, 33). Salvation by discipleship alone expects all those called to salvation to follow, learn from, and obey Jesus throughout their lives—no exceptions, no excuses.

THIS IS NOT ABOUT PERFECTION OR ANYTHING CLOSE TO IT

Just as Jesus calls us to the ideal, Paul writes in grand terms in Ephesians and Romans, as Eugene Peterson points out in his magnificent work *Practice Resurrection*. "Ephesians is a revelation of the church we never see. . . . The church we want becomes the enemy of the church we have."[14]

We don't live in the ideal; we live somewhere in the middle—in a world of confusion, struggle, weakness mixed with triumph. Even when Paul speaks of the great potential and power of life in union with Christ in Romans 6–8, he splays himself on the floor in chapter 7: "The trouble is with me, for I am all too human, a slave to sin. I don't really understand myself, for I want to do what is right, but I don't do it. Instead, I do what I hate" (Romans 7:14-15, NLT). Even Jesus' three most trusted disciples could not stay awake while he prayed, and Jesus himself acknowledges the gap between convictions and conduct: "The spirit is willing, but the body is weak" (Matthew 26:41, NLT).

We conclude with a review of Bonhoeffer's statement.

> The only man who has the right to say that he is justified by grace alone is the man who has left all to follow Christ. Such a man knows that the call to discipleship is a gift of grace, and that the call is inseparable from the grace.[15]

Salvation is by discipleship alone. It is time to wrestle with what that means. That begins with a basic principle: The only way you will experience the fullness of your salvation is through your own discipleship to Christ. Salvation can only be lived through discipleship, and if you don't live it, you don't have it.

YELLOW

I am only writing this to remember that I was not looking for a sign
And only realized hours later, as I turned the lever and felt the rush
of untested water which caught my breath, the surprise even
worse than the blast of cold on opening a shower door (such are
the pains of all sudden absences)
That the yellow-breasted bird sat like a needle in the haystack of
that brown, mottled wood
A coy reminder of something too quiet for words
A prophet whispering wordlessly, "yes, and keep moving forward"

1

THE DISCIPLE SHORTAGE

The harvest is great, but the workers are few.
So pray to the Lord who is in charge of the harvest;
ask him to send more workers into his fields.

MATTHEW 9:37-38, NLT

BILL

SO YOU ARE A RECIPIENT OF GOD'S FAVOR, of his grace—now what? You have been hanging around church and church people for a while now, maybe longer than a while. Emotional appeals are made at your church services and are a regular part of the church's weekly e-mails to the congregation: There is a disciple shortage. The shortage is ever present, and the nature of the appeals is sometimes desperate and guilt producing: "Volunteers are needed, or we will need to shut down this program." Getting enough people to care about something seems to be a challenge as old as the human race.

The Kingdom of God has now been around two thousand years. Jesus lived out his ministry years, was killed, was raised from the dead, appeared to his disciples and many others, and forty days after his resurrection, he left the earth to join his Father, leaving behind the commission to his followers to "Make disciples of all nations" (Matthew 28:19). He sent the Holy Spirit to be present with his followers throughout this period of Kingdom work. And yet, at all times in the two thousand years since the events of Jesus' earthly ministry, there has been a shortage of disciples. "The harvest is plentiful," Jesus told his first followers, "but the workers are few" (Matthew 9:37).

In a world population of nearly eight billion, there are approximately 2.5 billion professing Christians. The shortage of workers has grown exponentially with the population. Scholars who study cultures, population trends, and political realities acknowledge that finishing the great commission is a very complex mission. "Ask the Lord of the harvest, therefore," Jesus told his followers in light of this challenge, "to send out workers into his harvest field" (Matthew 9:38).

So why aren't you out there in the harvest field? Why don't you sense a personal responsibility to participate in the great commission of making disciples? Given the gospel that is most often preached in America, you probably don't think your salvation depends on it.

The gospel of cheap grace preaches that you can separate salvation from discipleship. Discipleship to Christ is broadly understood as a good idea, healthy for Christians, and you probably have considered and possibly even resolved to increase your commitment to the demands of discipleship. But life gets in the way, and when you don't get around to it, you face no real consequence.

In fact, we will be held accountable to God for our decisions and actions (Matthew 12:36; 1 Corinthians 3:12-15).

Only God can give you the desire to work for him, of course. But you are involved in the decision; there is nothing robotic about a relationship with God in Christ. The Scriptures call us to believe, to obey, to strive, to run with patience, to do hundreds of things that require an act of the will. We can make good decisions, we can make bad decisions; otherwise, there would be no need for commands or exhortations in Scripture. Thomas Aquinas described the interplay between God and human will: "For him [Aquinas], my actions are caused by God without ceasing to be free."[1]

Goodness can't be forced; you can't squeeze service out of a person. Paul put it so well:

> Work hard to show the results of your salvation,
> obeying God with deep reverence and fear. For God is
> working in you, giving you the desire and the power to
> do what pleases him.
>
> PHILIPPIANS 2:12-13, NLT

If you sense a nudge or even something stronger to move you from the safe confines of your comfort zone, it probably means that an activated disciple is praying for you. That person has seen the world and its helplessness, its confusion, its pain, its stubbornness through the eyes of Jesus and has decided to ask God to send you into the workforce. You should sense God's care for you, his interest in you, and his plan to send you into his world to love it like he loved it.

But before you can move ahead, you might need to change your mind. The predominant belief that becoming involved in God's mission is an act of extraordinary dedication is erroneous; the call to participate in the great commission is, in fact, absolutely normal—the logical act of a person who has been changed by the power of Christ.

TO CHANGE YOUR MIND

Jesus taught that salvation causes discipleship, just as certain as the sun on your face creates warmth. You are not just a Christian secure in Christ; you are a disciple of Christ, called to engage in his mission to the world (John 20:21). You are not placed on earth to simply live a good life; you are an ambassador for Christ, calling out to the world, "Be reconciled to God" (2 Corinthians 5:20). The first order of business is to reconfigure your thinking because that will determine what you do.

Charles Malik, former chairman of the UN Commission on Human Rights, once said that "if you win the whole world and lose the mind of the world, you will soon discover you have not won the world."[2] So what is it about the general thinking of church leaders and members that needs to change? Let's start with our message and our commission to distribute it to the world. What if Jesus didn't come back as he promised because we had preached the wrong gospel? A broken, upside-down gospel that filled the nations with Christians in name only? Charles Spurgeon, a great orator and pastor in nineteenth-century England, compared the gospel to a caged lion, arguing that it doesn't need to be defended; it just needs to be let out of its cage.[3] When priests and pastors decide how much of the gospel we get, when we get it, and under what conditions we get it, we cage our wild and dangerous story. We learn about the once-great lion when it was wild and free, but when we confront the words of Jesus, they disturb our theological categories and make us feel unsafe. For example,

> Not everyone who calls out to me, "Lord, Lord!" will enter the Kingdom of Heaven. Only those who actually do the will of my Father in heaven will enter. On judgment day many will say to me, "Lord! Lord! We prophesied in your name and cast out demons in your name and performed many miracles in your name." But I will reply, "I never knew you. Get away from me, you who break God's laws."
>
> MATTHEW 7:21-23, NLT

Generations of Christians have been programmed to believe that faith is no more than simple agreement with religious dogma. So it is a scandal to hear Jesus say, "Only those who actually do the will of my Father" are people of faith, the only ones who truly believe. The church has taught that no proof or actions are necessary to prove salvation, but Jesus here suggests that proof is required. This one factor could flip the gospel, our churches, our training, our creeds, and our worship upside down. Like Saint Francis, who allegedly threatened to stand on his head to make a point, we may need to stand on our heads to see the world aright.

The contemporary church is largely a church of effort, of showmanship, composed of well-meaning mission initiatives, but underlying it all is a nondiscipleship gospel.

Research shows that a large percentage of Christians never share their faith, which means they haven't joined the mission of Jesus in that formal way. The majority just want to survive their world, to avoid pain, shame, and failure. Wouldn't it be interesting if we required discipleship for church membership? I am sure there would be great rebellion among the church populace: "Someone has moved the goalposts! They are being legalistic; they are teaching works righteousness." In some ways, they would be right. Our default gospel has been drilled into the hearts and minds of congregations around the world for the last one hundred years. As the great Christian philosopher Dallas Willard stated, "As egg-headed as it may sound, our basic problem is our theology. The problem is our doctrine of salvation."[4]

THE NEW NORMAL

One of the things leaders do is define normal in a way that matches people's lived reality. Jesus was the master of such teaching, speaking in terms people understood and matching their experience to his insights. When you make a broad, general teaching for the masses, you want to keep it simple, you want to be clear, and you want to avoid extremes. Jesus' teaching at its simplest was this: "Follow me."

According to the missionary statesman Lesslie Newbigin,

The typical picture of the minister, at least in the
Protestant tradition, has been that of a teacher. He faces
the congregation as a teacher faces the class. They all,
preacher and people alike, have their backs turned to the
outside world. They face one another, and the minister
encourages, exhorts, and teaches. Many biblical pictures
portray Jesus in this relation to his disciples. The Italian
director Pasolini . . . in the film *The Gospel according to
St. Matthew* . . . shows Jesus going ahead of his disciples,
like a commander leading troops into battle. The words
he speaks are thrown back over his shoulder to the fearful
and faltering followers. . . . They all find their meaning
in the central keyword, "Follow me."[5]

Leaders lead; they are going somewhere, and those who
show interest in following them must ask questions on the run.
Jesus was usually walking, and it is often said that Jesus would
turn and respond to the those who would gather around him.
This is so different from contemporary leadership models, so
important, that it deserves an entirely different book.[6]

Jesus led with the core issue that could free people: *Following
me will cost you a lot—in fact, it will cost you everything you've got
. . . so really think about it!* Not the most market-tested statement
that would make people more likely to attend future meetings.
And yet we're told in the Scriptures that "a large crowd was following Jesus" (Luke 14:25, NLT). Holding back biblical teaching
of costly discipleship is not offering pastoral care to seekers; it's
pastoral malfeasance.

The great commission is built on the idea that disciples make other disciples who make still more disciples. Its genius is built on multiplication. When 96 percent of your disciples have been taught not to make disciples, you reap what you have sown.

EVERYONE MUST DECIDE

[Jesus said,] "If you want to be my disciple, you must, by comparison, hate everyone else—your father and mother, wife and children, brothers and sisters—yes, even your own life. Otherwise, you cannot be my disciple. And if you do not carry your own cross and follow me, you cannot be my disciple."

LUKE 14:26-27, NLT

Every person who follows Jesus does so because they want to. Jesus accepts no disciples who don't want to follow him. Any disciples who follow Jesus under compulsion are not his disciples and won't stick with him for long.

James and John dropped their fishing nets to follow Jesus because they were compelled to from deep within (Mark 1:19-20). In doing so, they left their father and their family business behind. As Bonhoeffer puts it, Jesus "bids him come and die."[7] When you are Jesus' disciple, what Jesus wants is the only thing that matters.

In Luke 14, Jesus sets the terms and conditions of discipleship: If you want to be Jesus' disciple, everything else places a distant second. He ends this declaration with "You cannot become my disciple without giving up everything you own" (Luke 14:33, NLT).

The reason Jesus wants everything from us is that he gave everything for us. Anything less would be a lousy deal. Holding back makes for bad marriages, poor business deals, terrible sports teams, disappointing art, cringeworthy poems and songs. Being partially committed to Christ is bad religion, and bad religion has done great damage to the world.

My neighbor once told me that he went to church because his wife and daughter wanted to, but he couldn't cope with the hypocrisy and lack of authentic compassion he saw in the church. I didn't attempt to defend the church against his charges. Instead, I answered, "When the church is bad, there is nothing worse, but when it is good, there is nothing better." That is why Jesus asks for everything.

IDOLS

When Jesus told his followers "You must, by comparison, hate everyone else," he didn't mean you are called to hate. Jesus' life and teaching were based on love, a commitment to others. The idea that hate is a recommended strategy is therefore easily dismissed. It is equally obvious, however, that he wants no rivals for control of your life.

Our deepest desires are revealed in our daily life and habits. One writer put it so well:

> Only about 5 percent of what we do in a given day is the outcome of conscious, deliberate choices we make, processed by that snowball on the tip of the iceberg that is human consciousness. The rest of our actions and behaviors are managed below the surface, by all sorts of learned yet now *un*conscious ways of intending and navigating the world.[8]

The overwhelming majority of our daily activities are done without thinking. They have been programmed into us by daily practices and habits, by family, culture, church, and life experience. The things that control our thinking and conduct, if they are not God—even otherwise good things, like family—are our idols. Only the one who can reach down into our hearts—the hearts he created and knows intimately—can override these unconscious patterns and change us (Jeremiah 17:9-10). God alone can get at our idols and remove them. He won't do that unless we are all in; God has chosen not to help us unless we submit to him.

There were three very powerful major idols during the time of Jesus, and they are still powerful today.

Materialist idols lead us to worship the physical universe, to the extent that unless something exists in material form, we suspect it is not real.

Idols of reason cause us to forget that reason doesn't have an independent existence; it is a human capability to be practiced, not a separate thing to be acquired. Moreover, our capacity for reason is inhibited by our humanness: Purely objective reason is impossible while we are finite—more so because we are fallen. The modern era, of course, elevated reason, giving hope to those who don't like the answers and explanations provided by a God who transcends our capacity for reason. In our idolatrous service to reason, we celebrated what can be repeatedly tested and verified and dismissed the ultimate questions of life—*What is the purpose of the universe? Why am I here? What does my life mean?*—as pointless pursuits. The idol of reason coaxes us away from these questions.

The third idol, *consumption*, dangles in front of us the joy and pleasure of new things. We enter the malls that are our temples of worship where the transactions are made by the priests or sales clerks who pretend to be interested in us and send us home with their personalized business cards. Our best friends are personal shoppers, maître d's and the valet-parking attendant.

There are other idols to consider. Two idols—*love* and *tolerance*—are almost identical twins. Idolatrous love is understood principally as a sentiment, not an action—identification with another person's success, failure, or tragedy rather than a conscious effort to benefit another. Tolerance—the uncritical acceptance of human differences and practices—thus becomes the highest form of love. What makes these particular idols illusive and dangerous is that they are close to being true. But all kinds of moral confusion can slip in under their protection.

One more idol deserves at least an honorable mention, and that is *production*. This is particularly common among leadership types. The drive to produce results and the rewards that come with those results are seductive and addictive.

These six idols are all contemporary threats moving in and out of our lives. Family, by contrast, is largely constant. We don't typically choose our families, and yet their impact on us, and our responsibilities to them, stay with us all our days. That is the reason Jesus calls us away from them.

FAMILY MUST NOT CONTROL YOUR LIFE

Worship of family is a serious problem, one that is exacerbated by trends in Western society. Families tend to stick together regardless of the facts. In many cases, familial blood runs thicker than the blood of Christ.

Noticing that the family unit was under threat from various

societal factors pulling people away from one another, the church began to teach that family comes first (after God, of course). Spouse first, children second, parents and siblings third, then it gets a bit fuzzy. A spirit of competition slowly crept into the church calendar and the family calendar.

Nothing brings this out more than when Christmas falls on Sunday. When Christmas Sunday becomes Christmas on Sunday, families must ask, "Do we go to church and adjust our family tradition, or do we keep our family traditions and skip church?" This entire discussion may seem trivial, and Jesus was certainly not setting up a competition between church life and family obligations. Rather, he was talking about allegiance: *what* controls you and *who* controls you.

Families are wonderful and maddening, supportive and destructive, right and wrong, restful and a war zone; you long for one and you want to run from it. The family is human, and its members have human desires, jealousies, needs, resentments, scores to settle, and stereotypical views of one another that are frozen in time. Family cannot be trusted to give you the right advice or to consistently be right, all your life, all the time. This is the reason Jesus mentions it. The contemporary family has much less influence on its members than it did in the early twentieth century. American families are less controlling because of the individualistic culture in which we live. When my wife and I were first married, we felt called to join an Athletes in Action basketball team. We had been married three months. The decision required us to drive from Oklahoma to California for a training conference, and we needed $300 to make the trip. Jane's mother would not loan us the money; she told us that if I wanted to preach, I could do so in Jane's hometown. Her family was not in favor of our running around the country preaching when it could be done in a normal way. So Jane's brother, Marc, loaned us the money, and we went on our way. This was a minor conflict if put in its proper context, but it was a big moment for us. Not for a moment did we consider not going. We could not stay—even if the entire family disowned us, we were ready to go. I am afraid that now, many people would give in to the family vote, afraid of a broken relationship with a parent or some other problem.

During Jesus' time, he disrupted families. James and John dropped their nets and left their father and mother behind, taking away the expectation that the sons would take over the family business and provide for the parents in their old age. It appears that James and John requested special places in heaven and were turned down. Their mother approached Jesus later and asked for special favors, ostensibly because she thought Jesus owed her family for taking her boys away (Matthew 20:20-28; Mark 10:35-45).

Jesus' own family heard rumors that he was not in touch with reality. His family feared for his life—and, of course, there was the issue of shame (Mark 3:20-21). But as Jesus said on another occasion, to the surprise of the crowds and especially our modern ears, "My mother and my brothers are all those who hear God's word and obey it" (Luke 8:21, NLT).

An even more pronounced difference between Jesus and his family occurred during a time of crisis and decision.

After this, Jesus traveled around Galilee. He wanted to stay out of Judea, where the Jewish leaders were plotting his death. But soon it was time for the Jewish Festival of

Shelters, and Jesus' brothers said to him, "Leave here and go to Judea, where your followers can see your miracles! You can't become famous if you hide like this! If you can do such wonderful things, show yourself to the world!" For even his brothers didn't believe in him.

Jesus replied, "Now is not the right time for me to go, but you can go anytime. The world can't hate you, but it does hate me because I accuse it of doing evil."

JOHN 7:1-7, NLT

Jesus' family's advice was to stop being an embarrassment. Or, in the case of his brothers, to take his embarrassment somewhere else: "Get lost!" It could be said the reason Jesus spoke first about the family's potential rivalry with the gospel is the fact that he knew he brought division between family members.

Don't imagine that I came to bring peace to the earth! I came not to bring peace, but a sword.

"I have come to set a man against his father,
    a daughter against her mother,
  and a daughter-in-law against her mother-in-law.
    Your enemies will be right in your own
        household!"

If you love your father and mother more than you love me, you are not worthy of being mine.

MATTHEW 10:34-37, NLT

Jesus received mixed messages from his family, especially his siblings. No one doubts that he loved them all, or that on occasion, he enjoyed their company. He was the oldest: He had spent the first thirty years of his life in the important position of firstborn son. He worked with his father until Joseph's death, and then he took on special responsibilities for his mother. Jesus is not antifamily; he is, however, clear on first allegiance, and he will not take second place. The only way one can be a disciple is to follow the leader. It is his advice, his approval, his wisdom and guidance that delivers a life in God's Kingdom. A life of joy and fulfillment, one of purpose and satisfaction and achievement and greatness in God's eyes.

Gladly, most families are supportive of their members striving for goodness and living out their dreams. I pray that you never need to be separated or estranged from family, but if you follow Jesus, it is likely to happen now and then.

SELF CANNOT CONTROL YOUR LIFE

First-century Palestine was far different from twenty-first century Western culture. A first-century person was identified by family. Even men's names indicated whose son they were and what city they hailed from: Jesus of Nazareth; Simon son of John. Regardless of the cultural packaging, something has remained the same: Humans want to have control of our lives—we want what we want, and we want it now (Jeremiah 17:9). Jesus put it plainly: "If you do not carry your own cross and follow me, you cannot be my disciple."

Again, this is not addressed to God's best and brightest, to a select elite; he was talking to a crowd. A crowd that was filled with a variety of attitudes. Some people were seriously interested, but others were skeptics; some were conflicted about what they were hearing, the same personality of many a thrill-seeking congregation. Jesus didn't hold back the high requirements; he was honest about what would be required. Earlier, he had been even more specific, again to a large crowd.

> If any of you wants to be my follower, you must give up your own way, take up your cross daily, and follow me. If you try to hang on to your life, you will lose it. But if you give up your life for my sake, you will save it.
>
> LUKE 9:23-24, NLT

Jesus is asking anyone who would follow him to enter a project that weans them off a life focused on self to a life focused on others. This is not quick or easy; it is a process that lasts a lifetime. But it is also a project that involves many milestones of changes and leaves the sweet taste of victory on one's lips.

A lifetime of discipleship is a lifetime of change, and often the change is difficult and painful. Moving your focus off yourself is the greatest challenge because self-indulgence is the strongest drug, and rehab is a way of life.

WEALTH CANNOT CONTROL YOUR LIFE

"You cannot become my disciple without giving up everything you own" (Luke 14:33, NLT). This is a jolting statement, especially if you have a lot! It might be even more startling if you don't have much and you must give that up too. But giving something up is very different from giving it away. This is an attitude; this is about how you view your wealth and for what purpose you use it.

If one were to simply think it through, this interpretation is obvious. The purpose of God is not for every wealthy person and family to simply give away all they have. There is a reason that certain people are wealthy and others are not. Some have abused the system; others have simply stolen the wealth. That was the case in the time of Jesus, as well. But the majority of Christian wealth is held by gifted and noble people who want to use it for God's purpose. If all the foundations gave away their principal wealth, and families and individuals did the same, it would be a disaster for the church and for the advancement of the gospel. The engine of the church's missional effort in 90 percent of the world is the wealth in North America. It would not be a good idea to take all the wealth accumulated by gifted and leading workers and hand it out to people who have no wealth, who don't know how to handle money or understand how to create more wealth. Wealth in the right hands multiplies; in the wrong hands, it disappears in a generation. The issue Jesus brings up is: What are you going to do with what you own? Is it mine, or yours? Jesus has confronted everyone with what it means to be a Christian, to follow him, to be his disciple. You cannot be his disciple unless you put Christ before your family, before yourself, and before your wealth. You must clear the decks of any rivals, of idols that would replace him.

Now that he has told us this, there is one more thing he asks of us.

COUNT THE COST

By virtue of asking everyone in the crowd to count the cost, Jesus sets himself apart from the majority of mainstream evangelicals in the twentieth and twenty-first centuries. Jesus asks this from the outset, but most of the church has tucked this bit of difficult news away for later. There seems to have been a general fear that asking too much too soon chases the seeker away. Perhaps we think people find a halfhearted commitment more appealing than something that would fully alter their lives. Obviously, Jesus had no fear that such a requirement would do anything other than enhance the lives of those within his hearing. Yes, he had followers abandon him. Yes, he even acknowledged that sometimes you can tell people too much (John 6:60-70; 16:12). But people who chose not to follow—not to join—were not his focus. He was more interested in those who did say yes, because then he would get a follower with eyes wide-open.

Isn't it obvious that Jesus equated belief with action, that faith is following, and that faith is only real in obedience—otherwise, it is not faith at all?

REPENTANCE

The English word *repentance* is derived from *metanoia*.[9] It means that after perceiving the facts, I change my mind. This is a work of the Holy Spirit; we can't make this happen on our own. But it does need to happen.

Jesus has asked the crowd to be really sure before they follow him, because this will be a full commitment, a full, unconditional surrender. He gives them two examples.

The first is the construction of a building: Make sure you have enough resources to finish the building. In an honor-shame society, you wouldn't want people laughing at you and shaming you for not being able to finish.

The second example is from the military: What is your troop strength? Do you have the number and type of soldiers who can win? Otherwise, run up the white flag and make peace (Luke 14:28-32).

Why does Jesus ask for so much? It is essential that his followers are fully committed because the stakes are so high. If there is something that we could unleash on the world worse than no Christians, it would be quasi-Christians: tepid, weak, and unconvincing people who won't change the world and at the same time convince the world that the church is a fraud.

> [Jesus said,] "Salt is good for seasoning. But if it loses
> its flavor, how do you make it salty again? Flavorless
> salt is good neither for the soil nor for the manure pile.
> It is thrown away. Anyone with ears to hear should
> listen and understand!"
>
> LUKE 14:34-35, NLT

This is one of the most vivid and straightforward rationales given by Jesus. In the Sermon on the Mount, Jesus said we are to be "the salt of the earth" (Matthew 5:13). In the first century, salt was used as a food preservative and, of course, to enhance the taste of food. If salt loses its taste, it is no good, not even for a manure pile. Jesus is uncomfortably clear: He is talking about a quasicommitted, halfhearted, semiobedient, self-indulgent church. He says that if you have spiritual ears, listen and understand (Matthew 11:15); I might add: He who has a nose, take a whiff! An unconverted church of nondisciples—"Christians" in name only—*stinks*. That church puts out a foul aroma, and no one wants to be in the vicinity.

We have a church populated with Christians who have been schooled in a nondiscipleship gospel, and we are paying the high cost of nondiscipleship. We have a built-in problem: The majority of people in the church have not counted the cost because they don't know about the cost. No one ever told them about repentance, about following, about putting aside their selfish ways, about taking up their cross, about dying in order to live, about giving in order to receive, about the joy of loving and serving others.

The consequences are quite serious: We will be stuck perpetually in a gospel that doesn't expect converts to participate in the greatest work on earth, the fulfillment of the great commission, of representing the Kingdom of God, of taking the Kingdom of God into other people's lives and living spaces. The gospels that are most often preached have taught the combined congregation that clergy are the stars and the populace is the supporting cast. The clergy perform, and the congregation applauds. Sunday after Sunday, fewer and fewer numbers gather to watch their stars ascend the platform to perform and display their gifts. The lights on the stage go up, the congregation settles down into their seats, and the lights go down over the crowd so that those on the platform can't see them. Congregations think the clergy's spiritual lives should be better than theirs, that they should pray more and live better, and that they are closer to God. Reaching the world is the clergy's job, and they won't change their minds until we change ours.

Jesus has called us, and when he calls, there is only one thing to do—follow him, and he will teach you everything you ever need to know. He calls you to salvation; that means you take up your cross, you start putting aside your selfish ways, you start walking behind him, with no conditions, no excuses, no negotiations. It means giving up the right to say no, it means living for others and, in doing so, finding yourself. It means not settling for a cheap substitute of salvation; namely, having your sins forgiven and obtaining the promise of heaven while you continue to live your banal life of meaningless production and consumption. Jesus promised us the good life: "The thief's purpose is to steal and kill and destroy. My purpose is to give them a rich and satisfying life" (John 10:10, NLT). Some translations call it an "abundant life." *Abundant* is something that exists in large quantities, something that is plentiful, profuse, rich, abounding, generous, bountiful, large, huge, lavish. So it is time to stop living an impoverished life, to give up on the paltry attempts you have made for meaning and joy, to throw it all away and follow Jesus. The now-famous, martyred missionary Jim Elliot once said, "He is no fool who gives up what he cannot keep to gain what he cannot lose."[10]

SOMETIMES DEATH IS NECESSARY

The celebration feels like birds landing on my open hands
But always flying off
Like trimming a bonsai tree with shears just too small
It's hard to get my heart around it all

Christmas comes blustery and red
With visions of sugarplums plump in our heads
But a day clothed in pastel?
And we are surrounded by so much spring
That the mystery is almost drowned out by our over-seeing and yet,
*   our not believing that*
The day that turns to night will turn to day again

But then I remember that
We pruned our rose-bushes two months ago
And that became its own Easter
I thought we killed them, but
The holy hush—not three days mind, you—but six, seven weeks
Turned them all to burning bushes
And it was too much metaphor
Life, life on every side, orange and red and white
The resurrection and the life

We are destined to walk, if we will, as he once walked,
In the cool of a garden
Up a long, lonely trail
Into the perfect sacrifice of love which keeps whispering,
"Sometimes death is necessary,
Keep walking, still"

2

THE UPSIDE-DOWN KINGDOM

BUILDING DISCIPLE-MAKING CULTURES

"Come, follow me," Jesus said.

MATTHEW 4:19

BRANDON

RECLAIMING THE GOSPEL MEANS making Jesus' call to "Follow me" normative. This reality of a gospel that demands discipleship and transformation is like the headwaters of the entire salvation enterprise. God is the God who makes all things new, and all things new means transformation (Revelation 21:5). As Paul says, "What counts is the new creation" (Galatians 6:15). Paul understood that what happened in Christ was the coming of a new world, ever breaking into our own. Though all creation longs for this transformation—redemption from its decay into glorious liberty—the transformation starts within us (Romans 8:21). So Jesus says, "The kingdom of God is in your midst" (Luke 17:21).

From these headwaters—a gospel that makes discipleship and transformation (not just church membership) normative—we can move midstream, to the creation of disciple-making culture, which is the focus of this chapter.

Culture is the stuff you don't have to think about it. It's made up of the stuff that is normative. I didn't wake up this morning and debate whether I should eat with a knife and a fork or chopsticks, because in our house the culture is a knife and a fork. Most of the norms in our culture we never think about: When I meet someone on the street for the first time—say, a friend of a friend—I reach out and shake their hand. I do the same thing when I'm at church, but it's not unusual to hug someone there—even on a second or third interaction—because our church culture is big on hugging. On such norms and subconscious intuitions and understandings, culture is built.

The culture Jesus was building would assume that the gospel

necessarily involves transformation—namely, allegiance to Jesus as Lord and a new way of living because of it—and so discipleship would be normative. For the early church, this was stuff they didn't have to think about. Given our distance from that early-gospel culture, we have to think about it, so in this chapter, we will attempt to bridge the distance by considering the language, metaphors, and foundational thinking around a gospel centered in discipleship. In other words, how do we create cultures in which discipleship is as normative as using a knife and a fork or chopsticks, hugging or shaking hands?

CREATING CULTURE: THE LANGUAGE WE USE

Creating disciple-making culture means focusing on language. Culture is created by the language we use and what we celebrate.[1] In later chapters, we will discuss creating culture through what we celebrate, but first, it is necessary to define terms. We must go upstream to define central language—words like *gospel* and *discipleship*—because misunderstandings upstream play out in critical ways downstream. We have to make it clear what we mean by discipleship and disciple making. This doesn't happen in a vacuum; in reclaiming these words, we are working against powerful but misguided contemporary notions of what discipleship is. People describe being a disciple as "going to church" or even just "being a Christian." Those two phrases are so watered-down, meaning so many different things depending on who is using them, as to approach uselessness. If we want to create a culture in which discipleship is normative, we will have to flesh out what a disciple is, according to Jesus.

LANGUAGE CREATES REALITY

Starbucks provides a great example of using language to invite people into a new way of thinking. When I'm in my local (non-Starbucks) coffee store, I often ask for a "grande." To which the barista replies, "You mean a medium?" "Oh, right," I say, ". . . yes, a medium." Starbucks, to create a culture in which people thought about coffee in a new way—as an exotic experience—and to claim mind share in the world of competitive coffee, imported Italian language (and threw in "tall") to denote its sizes: tall, grande, venti. To build a distinct culture for Starbucks, the company incorporated language that has become, for some, a normative way of thinking about ordering coffee. This changes the experience of the consumers, whether they are conscious of it or not. That's the power of language: It creates a normative way of thinking within us.

Churches aren't businesses, and Christian leaders are not business leaders, but they are fighting for mind share; they must capture the attention and the imagination of those who follow them. Our lingua franca matters. Our vernacular—the language we use most naturally and normatively—reveals how we view reality. In the early church, the phrase "Jesus is Lord" was a loaded one that flew in the face of the dominant culture. It was a call to a revolutionary way of living based not in empire but in God's Kingdom. It was, in fact, treasonous language. It was far more potent than what we now mean by "being a Christian," which can mean anything from being a sincere and devoted follower of Jesus to being born into a Christian home.

I cringe when I hear people say, "I go to church at Long Beach Christian Fellowship." I know what is meant by the phrase, and

I don't make a fuss over it, but think about the reality that phrase invokes: I *go* there, to church, then I leave. It creates the idea—and a culture around the idea—that church is a place we go to rather than the reality of a people on a journey and a mission together. In the New Testament, "church" is presented as a people doing life together (see Acts 2:42-47), learning to honor and love one another (Romans 12:10). It is a qualitative reality, based on a way of being together. Our language, on the other hand, often encourages a consumer mind-set, not a mind-set of participation. I coach people to use the language "I'm a part of LBCF" or "I'm a part of the community (or family) at LBCF." This language invites an entirely different reality than "going to church." By the same token, we don't call our worship gatherings "services": Although it had a beautiful intent in its earlier usage, evoking worship as an act of love and service to God, this word has become eroded through time and imagination to mean very little other than a religious liturgy. Instead, we call them "gatherings" or even "family gatherings." This change in language invites an entirely different world of meaning, imagination, and possibility.

Language, used powerfully, can always call people into a new reality. It can build new culture. Of course, if people cling to thinking of church as a place they go rather than a community that they embody, changing the language will have little effect. Still, language is a good place to start.

TOWARD A NEW NORMAL

The gospel, as we will unpack in future chapters, is the Good News that Jesus is the King who makes all things new and who invites us to follow him into the good life.

I have sat in rooms with discipleship thought leaders and

realized, *Wait, what Person A means by* discipleship *is clearly not what Person B means.* One uses the word synonymously with mentoring, but the other uses it as "everything we do in church is discipleship, if it points to Jesus." Obviously, we can't have an on-point conversation if there's confusion over basic terms. You can't build any culture around something you can't define and describe.

What, then, do we mean by the language *discipleship* and *disciple making*? Discipleship, simply, is a process of transformation by which we learn to live and love like Jesus. It is the process by which God's Spirit is formed in us such that we come to look like Jesus (2 Corinthians 3:18). Disciple making is the process by which this transformation spreads from individual to individual and becomes a movement that multiplies. This gets us closer to language around which culture can be built, but we need to be more precise. On a granular level, what exactly do we mean by *disciple*?

A disciple is one who follows Jesus into the good life. Into the abundant life.

This simple definition of *disciple* does two things: (1) It makes it clear that being a disciple is not just going to heaven when you die but rather focuses on life here and now; and (2) It points to the reality that we aren't going to heaven when we die but rather that heaven is coming here (Revelation 21:1-5). And it elicits an obvious question: Well, what *is* the good life?

Left to our predominant cultural understandings, we might think that the good life is about amassing wealth or fame or accruing power. But to Jesus, the good life is certainly not about the American dream. And what it is exactly must be fleshed out. It's in this fleshing out that such language, ultimately, can help create a disciple-making culture. If we can be precise about what the good life is, as Jesus taught it, we can create cultures that embrace what Jesus values, and we can create disciples who embody those values.

THE GOOD LIFE

So, let's explore a bit: What is the good life, according to Jesus? Paul points to it in Ephesians 2:10: a life of doing good work that God himself prepared for us to do. Jesus called it the abundant life. Perhaps we should ask: How did Jesus understand the good life, in concert and contrast with his contemporaries (give or take a few centuries)? This will help us see how Jesus drew on the best cultural thinking of his day while nevertheless interjecting a completely new model of what true goodness is and how it is formed in us.

SOCRATES AND PLATO

Socrates (for whom Plato speaks) and Plato call "the good life" an examined life. Socrates famously said, "The unexamined life is not worth living."[2] In other words, the good life meant using reason to rein in your passions, to live a harmonious life, by which you could gaze on reality and be captivated and transformed by the truly beautiful and eternal realities beyond the ever-changing material universe.[3] This reining-in-of-passion-through-reason is a key theme in Greek philosophy. In simplest terms, we can understand the idea by an illustration: "Eating three cupcakes tastes good, but it leads to bad consequences; therefore, I will eat only one cupcake." You must be free of the whims of your desire to pursue and contemplate what really matters (truth, goodness, beauty) rather than experiencing unpleasantness (in this case, throwing up in the bathroom).

To help us understand the role of reason in human life, Socrates divides man into two parts, represented by two horses: One, "Appetite," is stubborn. The other horse, "Spiritedness," can be controlled by reason and can rein in appetite. If someone doesn't make use of reason to control spirit, the appetite will carry the chariot all over the place, with disastrous results. But when someone reins in their passion, they can live a harmonious life and be useful to their community and the state. Inward harmony, or justice (Greek root *dikaiosuné*, found often in the New Testament and, in this context, denoting right moral action and behavior[4]), will translate into the harmonious operation of the state.

With this definition in mind, we ask: What in Plato's and Socrates's teaching is in concert with Jesus' teaching about the good life? We see much that resonates:

- the life of the soul matters (Matthew 16:26; John 11:25);
- this internal truth matters more than external appearance or an appearance of truth (Matthew 23:26); and
- it's not just the individual who matters but the collective (the New Testament is in constant tension between the individual work of salvation and its communal nature).

What, in Plato (and Socrates), contrasts with Jesus' teaching? Very simply, Plato's division between body and spirit (he went so far as to describe the soul as imprisoned in the body[5]) finds little correlation with Jesus' notion of man as a unified whole—body, mind, soul, and spirit, at the center of which is heart. Plato's dualistic division between body and mind set up Western thought for extreme dualism and the belief that the material world is bad (ultimately exemplified in Gnosticism), whereas Hebrew thought continued to emphasize the inherent goodness of physical life and the material world. The world may be marred by sin, but it is still the realm of God's work of redemption. This belief naturally leads one toward taking good action in God's beautiful world rather than trying to escape it.[6] There is little notion that the material universe is bad or evil, as you find in Gnostic Greek thought. These ideas play out in tangible ways and show up even in the division between conversion and discipleship. For example, what matters to many Western Christians is "being a Christian" (conversion) who is "going to heaven"—the material world is bad, after all, so let's get out of here and get to heaven—but not necessarily "following Jesus" (discipleship) in *this* world. If our mind-set is thoroughly Greek, we will have little place for thinking of discipleship as "embodied participation in the new creation" (to use Matthew Bates's description).[7] This idea of an embodied spirituality flows from a Hebraic worldview.

ARISTOTLE

In Aristotle, we find the idea that in living virtuously, you'll experience *eudaemonia*, often translated as "flourishing,"[8] which is very close to the biblical notion of shalom. According to Aristotle, this flourishing is the one thing that all people seek.[9] It is a self-justifying good, an end in its own right. *Eudaemonia* doesn't come through meeting one or two desires or experiencing thrills of pleasure (says Aristotle, "one swallow does not make a summer") but by the many choices that make up a good life.[10] In his *Nicomachean Ethics*, he says we must cultivate the virtues, the virtuous always being the middle ground between two extremes.[11] Courage, for example, is the balance between cowardice and recklessness, just as generosity is the golden mean between being stingy and being wasteful. This golden mean is Aristotle's practical guide for how to behave. Every good choice, he says, is a good choice between two bad extremes.

What, then, is in concert between Aristotle and Jesus? Well, the idea that practical ethics in everyday life matters is central to both Aristotle and Jesus. For Aristotle, it's the golden mean; for Jesus, it's the Golden Rule (Matthew 7:12).

And what, in Aristotle, contrasts with Jesus' teaching?

Like Plato, Aristotle emphasizes contemplation, and he says that "God," as we must think of him, is an "Unmoved Mover," the first cause that causes all other existence. His God or first principle is quite impersonal. The Unmoved Mover cannot, for example, experience passion, because that would mean he experiences lack (desire that moves us is always connected to something we lack), which is impossible for a perfect being.[12]

God as the Unmoved Mover is entirely different from the picture of God we get in Hebrew thought, where God is fully passionate, the Most Moved Mover. And in Jesus, against this notion of an impersonal Unmoved Mover we get Jesus' picture of God (Jesus himself being the perfect picture of God) who is supremely concerned and supremely moved (e.g., Matthew 23:37; Luke 12:7; John 11:35).

STOICISM

Stoicism, which became the dominant philosophical system in the Roman Empire, accepted much of Plato and Aristotle's philosophy and emphasized aligning with the harmony—the *Logos*—found in nature. To live a good life is to live in harmony with the natural world, which, as we've mentioned, can be achieved through the right regulation of our whims and desires and a proper focus on detached contemplation. When we die, if we have lived well, we can return to the harmony of nature.

Stoicism had a significant influence on early Christian thought (the Logos language of John 1 draws on Stoic ideas before transcending them), but the big difference between Jesus' teaching and Stoicism is twofold.

First, to the Stoics, the world was an endless cycle of natural processes; to a Jewish mind like Jesus', history was not a cycle but a line with a clear beginning (Creation) and, ultimately, an endpoint (the redemption of all things). As Rabbi Lord Jonathan Sacks, former chief rabbi of the United Synagogue in Britain, says, the great breakthrough of Jewish thought was seeing God in history, not just in nature, as the Stoics did.[13] God doesn't merely set the cycles of nature in motion; he acts *in* history, to lead all of history to redemption. Because of this, God is not some impersonal force or an Unmoved Mover but a passionate God of love and holiness who engages the whole of creation. Jesus and the gospel's teaching fully accord with this Hebraic worldview and the sacredness of time. After all, in the fullness of time, "God sent his Son" (Galatians 4:4).

Second, and this cannot be overstated: Jesus' promise of eternal life is far greater than just returning as atoms into the harmony of nature. Jesus invited us into life that never dies, in this world and in the world to come. He offers hope in a way that Roman philosophy never could, for a tangible knowledge of God transforms life in this world and promises unending life in a world to come (e.g., John 4:14).[14]

JESUS' CONTEMPORARIES (JEWISH LEADERS)

And what about the Jewish leaders of Jesus' day? They were diverse, of course. Pharisees had different beliefs than Sadducees, for example, and the sect at Qumran had a different way of life, as well. But the belief that united them all was that the good life was found in devotion to God expressed in concrete action in daily life. Such action kept you pure, preserving you for God amid a treacherous world.

Faith was faithfulness to the Torah and the traditions (though the Torah was interpreted in different modes, and the traditions varied from group to group).

Jesus, too, focuses on the practical, loving action we take in everyday life (e.g., Matthew 25:40). But what is so different in Jesus' teaching is that the good life isn't about performing well enough to curry God's favor, which is the sense you get from many of Jesus' contemporaries. Instead, Jesus focuses on the blessing of spiritual poverty, which robs us of having any pretense before God or man. For this reason, he focuses on hypocrisy (the embodiment of pretense), the right use of money (the love of which can blind us to our true poverty), and the need for forgiveness (which we cannot admit if we are stuck in pretense). In his teaching, he focuses not on outer appearance but on inner transformation. Jesus, for example, says, "You have heard . . . 'You shall not commit adultery.' But I tell you that anyone who looks at a woman lustfully has already committed adultery with her in his heart" (Matthew 5:27-28).

He abandons external purity codes and focuses on a changed heart and life, because you don't become good through religious performance but rather by becoming open and undone before God.

Jesus begins the Sermon on the Mount, for example, by declaring that blessed are "the poor in spirit"—those who are broken and needy and who *know* they are broken and needy (Matthew 5:3). This is a complete reorientation to the starting point of spiritual life, with an end goal not of looking good but instead of knowing you're *not* good nor can you be, in and of yourself. This means rethinking the entire purpose of the Jewish law within spiritual life. The law is given not to make you good but to show you that you can *never* be good on your own (Romans 7:1-13). The law, then, produces a crisis: It reveals that we can't be transformed through performance and instead must become open to God on a much deeper level of heart, soul, and mind.

Jesus, in this vein, sums up the entire law by saying, "Love God with everything you have, and love others as you love yourself" (Mark 12:30-31, author's paraphrase). Jesus quotes the book of Deuteronomy (6:5) to make it clear that the good life is not something newfangled but is instead an ancient, deeply rooted idea. Yet still, the power to live into this reality comes not from our own willpower but from emptying before God, acknowledging weakness, need, and dependence. That emptying is the only way you become, as Dallas Willard said, the kind of person who "naturally does good."[15] Jesus, then, completes the work of the prophets who came before: It's not about religion, he says, but about a transformed heart.

Again, in this way, Jesus is in accord with Plato, focusing on inner transformation as a highest concern—and transformation that expresses itself for the good of the world. But Jesus' notion of how this transformation comes about is different in a way Plato could never conceive. It comes through an intimate and highly personal contemplation and experience of a personal God who is at once transcendent (out there) but also immanent (right here), in infinite goodness. God is not an impersonal being in a world of forms, as Plato's God is, nor distant and impassable, as we find in Aristotle's Unmoved Mover, or more a force than a being, as we find in the Stoics, but a God of immanent personality, in whom there is real, tangible grace and love.[16] When we see and receive this love, we are changed not through the mere contemplation of ideas but through spiritual power available concretely in a personal deity. This is why the New Testament focuses so closely on grace, which, in its broadest sense, is the empowering manifestation of God's deeply personal love.

The good life is about becoming open to this personal Creator-God. This openness is far harder to live into than merely being pious or religious. It requires transparency and vulnerability with God (about our passions and our weaknesses), and such vulnerability can only be fully experienced in community with others. Christianity requires joining a community of people based not on image, power, or prestige but on vulnerable humility and honesty about our human weakness. "You must have the same attitude that Christ Jesus had" (Philippians 2:5, NLT; see verses 5-8). An attitude of considering others better than yourself. Of honoring them. It's only in this posture of humility with each other that we can fully experience God. We do it practically, face-to-face. Much as God became incarnate and face-to-face with us, we see God as we are face-to-face with one another. ("If we don't love people we can see, how can we love God, whom we cannot see?" [1 John 4:20, NLT].) We embrace and do not forsake each other amid our weaknesses, just as God does for us. In this way, we create a "community of prayerful love," in which God's presence is known.[17] And we fulfill Jesus' hopeful prophecy: "Your love for one another will prove to the world that you are my disciples" (John 13:35, NLT).

IN THE ROMAN WORLD

What about the empire of which Jesus and his contemporaries were uncomfortably a part? Again, volumes could be (and have been) written about the concept of "the good life" in the Roman Empire. And while they had elaborate philosophical notions of summum bonum ("the supreme or highest good"), in practical terms, the Romans were all about power.[18] How else, after all, does one take over the known world but by concentrating on power? Even the word *virtue*, which we associate with inner attributes of courage or mercy or honesty, is rooted in the Latin word for "virility." In the brutal world of the Roman Empire, it was about being the man on top. A Roman paterfamilias ("the father of a family"), in whom was concentrated all the power of the household, could basically do what pleased him.[19] He could have sex with whomever he wanted, for example.

What was so radically different about Jesus' teaching was that true power came not in external displays of strength (legions and military victories and symbols of triumph) but in love and humility and sacrifice. After all, in Christian thought, God becomes a battered and crucified human being, foolishness to the Greeks (and absurdity to the Romans; 1 Corinthians 1:23). Christianity changed everything. In our world, we care about the poor and the powerless and the victimized precisely because God himself cares about victims and even allowed himself to become a victim. Jesus confronts violence not with more violence but with forgiveness.[20] The revolution that happened in Jesus, which literally changed the world, cannot be overstated.

WHAT ABOUT US?

Let's jump forward two thousand years. What about us? What is the good life in contemporary American society? Obviously, material wealth and success are considered important. But the mantras at the center of American life now are "you be you" and "you do you." As long as you aren't hurting anyone else, you get to declare who you are and what you are about. As Jonathan Sacks puts it: "We [have moved] from a world of 'We' to one of 'I': the private pursuit of personal desire."[21] Jonathan Haidt describes this new liberal morality as being fair and doing no harm.[22] As we will explain further in chapter 4, the dominating cultural narratives now are:

1. *the Identity narrative*: You've got to be true to yourself;
2. *the Freedom narrative*: You should be free to live any way you want, as long as you're not harming anyone;
3. *the Happiness narrative*: You should do what makes you happy, because the point of life is to enjoy it; and
4. *the Morality narrative*: No one has the right to tell anyone what is right or wrong for him or her.[23]

I recently read a short article on Janelle Monáe's sexuality (and I confess, I really had no idea who Monáe was). The author, in describing Monáe's coming out as pansexual, writes, "For those of you who might be confused by Monáe's fluid and nuanced sexual identity, let us remind you that it is her right to identify however she pleases at any time she chooses."[24] I'm not here to comment on Monáe's sexual identity (usually a foolhardy enterprise outside of a personal relationship with someone) but rather to point out that, philosophically and culturally, this sort of statement is now at the center of our practical ethics. A sobering thought. The author's statement is spoken from such authority, not to mention condescension ("Let us remind you . . ."), but there is little notion—in this statement or the entirety of the article—of the value of authenticity beyond authenticity for authenticity's sake. And, as my friend Bryan Rouanzoin says, "Authenticity without commitment is just self-indulgence."[25] If our highest aim is simply authenticity without any larger cultural narrative of what's meaningful or beautiful— if authenticity is understood as an aim in and of itself—we have devolved into a pretty threadbare notion of the good life.[26]

In a profound way, of course, the idea of self-expression is a very Christian message. Jesus freed us, as God freed the Israelites from slavery, as God sent Adam and Eve into the world to flourish (Genesis 1:28), which *does* mean an authentic expression of self. But in Christian thought, true flourishing does not happen outside the context of losing your life for something greater than yourself (Matthew 10:39). In other words, "you do you" is not a Christian imperative. Becoming something for others— life, love, kindness, mercy—very much is. Transformation does not happen simply by expressing yourself but by expressing the best in you for the sake of others.

So what, then, is Jesus' definition of the good life? How would we summarize Jesus' unique perspective on what constitutes the good life? If we want to be clear about what a disciple is, to create culture in which discipleship and disciple making are normative, we need to answer these questions. As we said above, the good life, in Jesus' thinking, is a life that is continually becoming open to God, which is how we become *like* God. So we must ask, "Well, what did Jesus do?" Let us return then to Jesus' simple summation of the good life (and, therefore, of discipleship): To be like Jesus means (1) loving God with everything within you; and (2) loving others as God does, even more than you love your own self (Mark 12:30-31).

The good life is a great emptying, born in love, of a personal God and of specific people. It is a life of growing compassion and empathy. It is, simply, about learning to love as God loves. Any discipleship practice that does not ultimately lead to a great expression of *hesed*—of loving-kindness[27]—in the world is not actually a discipleship practice. Greater understanding of the Bible is a wonderful thing, but information download can actually impede and not abet spiritual growth.

This, on one hand, seems obvious, a true "duh" moment. Of course it's about love; it always is. But on the other hand, when compared with the other systems of thought, Jesus' teaching stands in stark contrast because it is always a path of descent— an emptying of self that requires a confession of weakness. And it is a movement of personal, transforming love within us that demands that we love others. Plato and Aristotle and the Stoics focus on coming into harmony with the forms of nature. It is very much an internal harmony, with the focus on the harmony of our own soul. The Judaism of Jesus' day, at least among its competing sects, overfocused on personal religious performance, which is another type of inward focus. Our contemporary culture focuses on the most authentic expression of our inner life. But Jesus sidesteps all that inner-focused energy by creating disciples who are always moving outward, for the sake of others. This is how you know they are, in fact, disciples of Jesus (John 13:35).

All this is possible because God is not an impersonal force (contra Plato and Aristotle and the Stoics) but a God who is utterly concerned with life here and now, in a historical story that is leading somewhere—to redemption (contra the Stoics). And because what matters to God is not external religious performance (contra the power center of Judaism in Jesus' day), or power (contra the Romans), or self-expression (contra our contemporary mantras) but a life being transformed to love as God loves, for the sake of others. It is about action in the world for the sake of the world, because that's what God does, and we are becoming like God himself.

This is life in an upside-down Kingdom, to use Dallas Willard's phrase.[28] Willard gave us the image of a pilot who thinks she's flying right-side up when she's actually upside down. We do the same, thinking we are flying upright—just being normal humans, focused on power and prestige and performance and perhaps thinking God is distant, an impersonal force. God calls us to lose all, to lose what we think is valuable, to learn to fly right-side up. It *feels* upside down to us because such an emptying into divine love feels incredibly vulnerable. Love means we will lose, and we know it. We don't love God because we know that in encountering God's love, there will be suffering, a loss of control. That's exactly what suffering is, after all: It's being out of control when we want to be in control. To live in an upside-down Kingdom means to give ourselves to love anyway. To recognize Jesus is flying right-side up and that, ultimately, if we follow him, he will lead us into the resurrection pattern in which what we thought of as life (power, prestige, and performance) is revealed as the dust it is, and what we thought was death (suffering for the sake of love) is actually unending life. For "if you try to hang on to your life, you will lose it. But if you give up your life for my sake, you will save it" (Matthew 16:25, NLT).

INTO THE GOOD LIFE: A LIFE OF ABUNDANT LOVE

To be very clear, the only way to develop this outward energy of love is through intentional inward focus. Jesus often withdrew to the wilderness to pray by himself, withdrawing, in some sense, into himself. But this movement inward always flowed into a movement outward. All spiritual practice is about becoming people who love as God loves. The sort of people who lay down their lives for others.

In the Gospels, we constantly see Jesus train his disciples to love. For example, in the Gospel of Luke, the disciples debate about who will be the greatest in the Kingdom of God (Luke 22:24-30). This is the inner movement that lives in all of us: "How am I doing? Am I significant? Will I be noticed?" And what does Jesus do? He tells them, "You guys are having a conversation like those who don't know God. And anyway, God's not like that at all. If you want to be great, serve others" (author's paraphrase). Notice what the Master Disciple Maker does: Jesus takes his disciples out of the universal conversation about "How am I doing?" and directs them to a new reality: "God is entirely more good than anything you are familiar with so far." From this notion of God's unsurpassed goodness, Jesus directs them to a new question: "How are you doing loving others?" This is the constant pattern of discipleship (the good life) in Scripture:

How am I doing? → Do you see how very good God is (he pursues you even when you're unfaithful)? → How are you giving your life for others (as God does for you)?

Another way to say "How are you giving your life for others?" is "How are you becoming like God?" because giving his life away is what God is always doing.

In our language, then, if we are to follow Jesus, we must make it clear that when talking about discipleship, we are talking about growing in empathy and compassion. We are not just talking about external religious performance but about internal transformation. We are talking about a change in how we love, in practical terms. And not only will we need to describe this movement of grace in us becoming grace moving through us, but we will need to identify practices that can help us become open to God and to love like God, since that is at the center of discipleship as Jesus describes it.

FULL PICTURE OF A DISCIPLE

To make a disciple-making culture more normative, we need language that makes it clear what a disciple is, in accordance with Jesus' teaching of the good life. How do we bring this ancient language to contemporary relevance? Here's an example from our church. Our language is no perfect rendering or a silver bullet, but I offer it here simply as an example. Because all leaders, be they Howard Schultz or a local pastor or a Christian leader, must find language that is potent and effective in his or her unique context.

A disciple lives the good life by:

- abiding in his or her **adoption in God** (a life of radical grace);
- living as an **ambassador of the Kingdom of God**, participating with God to see all things made new (a life of radical mission); and
- pursuing an **abundant life** through listening and responding to God's Spirit in things big and small (a life of radical obedience and generosity).

While these three points don't capture everything about Christian life (for example, all of this happens in the context of community), they provide a good road map around which other important markers can orient.

Our discipleship language needs to be potent, and it needs to invite people into a story in which following Jesus is the normal expectation for all Christians. The language of adoption points people, for example, to a relational—not a transactional—notion of salvation. The language of ambassadorship makes it clear that our following Jesus extends to where we live, work, and play. And the language of abundance and obedience reinforces the idea of faith as allegiance, that Jesus is not only our Savior but also our Lord.

There are all sorts of ways to summarize and put into powerful language Jesus' picture of discipleship, and it will vary from context to context. But at the heart of whatever language we choose, we must recontextualize salvation not as "going to heaven when you die" but as being in a transforming relationship with the God who is all life and love. It must paint a picture of the good life that is fully embodied and actively participating in God's work in the world. It must invite people to be transformed by love. With such language in hand, we can form a wide foundation for vibrant disciple-making cultures.

DOWNSTREAM

This review of the language and underlying worldview of the gospel culture Jesus built, and the alternative visions that compete for its primacy in our contemporary imagination, sets a baseline for how we can assess the current cultural climate. What is getting between us and Jesus' discipleship gospel? In the chapters that follow, we'll assess the contemporary cultural rivals to the discipleship gospel and their impact. Then we'll be ready to consider practices that recover the subversive, transformative gospel that Jesus presented us with.

GOOD FRUIT

There is something gained, of course, in the glad reality that
I can peel and pierce an orange whenever I like (or twice, or thrice)
Can walk or bike to the grocery and engorge on citrus
With fine happy fingers or the expectant knife

But one hundred fifty years ago, a woman walked six miles to town
And waited two hours for a train, late at the gate from a broken beam,
Which finally lumbered and gave out, with a great sigh of steam,
After a trail too long, a master mean

And from a car she watched, as they hauled though the yard
Mail and bundles and boxes large, and a sack of fruit
Which, ten minutes later, in the general store, she made sure
Was first unpacked and, laying her hands on two—the limit—
She paid bright coins for that good booty, then walked back
    the six miles
A smile in each step

All to bring her girl a gift, a Magi, a wise woman
And the girl gaped
As if the skies peeled back and angels sang, at the sight of that
    orange orb
All on Christmas day

There's something gained in that story, too,
The beauty of effort, the perfection of simple things
When you still have eyes to see miracles all around you
And the soul's longing is longer, made more sure by how it finds you
And what it will require of you

And something lost, too, in how easily I weigh and peel the things
Or throw away the ones which fail to please
Because, after all, life is hard, and it's often hard because it's easy
And easy doesn't please me, or you, or us
With these souls meant for good, hard work
To fill the earth, subdue it,
And bring of our lives sweet, good fruit

3

THE GOSPEL AMERICANA

The conflict about Christianity will no longer be doctrinal conflict. . . .
The conflict . . . will be about Christianity as an existence. . . .
The rebellion in the world shouts: We want to see action!

STEPHEN BACKHOUSE, *KIERKEGAARD: A SINGLE LIFE*

Americana refers to artifacts . . . related to the history, geography,
folklore and cultural heritage of the United States.

ART & ANTIQUES MAGAZINE

BILL

A YOUNG PASTOR WAS TAKING a graduate-school course on the Gospel of Mark. He was required to read the Gospel twelve times and make notes before his first class. On the first day of class, he raised his hand. "I have read the Gospel twelve times as assigned, I have made notes, and I have reflected on it a great deal. Why is it called the Gospel of Mark? I could not find any gospel in it."

Nowhere in the Gospel of Mark will you find a plan of salvation—what most of us today consider the totality of "the gospel." But the plan of salvation is an invention of the twentieth-century American church, a three- to five-step formula engineered to produce decisions for Christ.[1] To be more accurate, it doesn't create decisions, but rather *more* decisions, and more predictable decisions. If the young man would have found a gospel tract tucked between pages of the Gospel of Mark, he would have said, "Ah, I've found it: Here is the gospel. I have it in my hand."

Americana is the term we use to describe distinctly American cultural artifacts or phenomena. As such, to take an extract from the gospel and condense it to a cliché or motto and make it easier for people to jump in is Americana at its finest: steps, laws, pathways, a bridge, or a ladder—let's get it done, count it, seal it, baptize it.

This distinctly American plan of salvation has replaced the metanarrative of Scripture, from creation to consummation, with a new category of Christianity: a technical salvation, a conversion event. It also has left in its wake millions of nominal Christians who can be counted but can't be counted on.

An artifact is an object made by a human being. Cultural artifacts range from surfboards to electric guitars. Artifacts are reflective of the culture in which they are made. In that vein, it can be a helpful exercise to think of "gospels" as artifacts: Jesus presented a gospel that was born of the biblical vision of the world. In my book *Conversion and Discipleship*, I have identified five alternative gospels that are artifacts of our culture.[2] Each of these gospels reshapes the lives of Christians and, by extension, the watching world. The various gospels are:

1. forgiveness only;
2. gospel of the left;
3. prosperity gospel;
4. consumer gospel; and
5. gospel of the right.

The focus here is what each of these gospels creates. As we explain that, it will reveal what these gospels naturally lead to and how they have failed us.

THE GOSPEL OF FORGIVENESS PRODUCES ONLY PASSIVITY

A gospel reduced to forgiveness of sins doesn't create passivity in every convert. But then again, it doesn't have to: A simple majority is enough to rip the heart out of the collective group. By passivity, we don't mean inaction, for many professors of Christ are activists. While the abuse of grace does create a considerable passivity in a large swath of the church, its effect is more in attitude. It is the posture people take or are taught once they have been introduced in the Christian stream. Often, the idea of grace is that there is nothing left to do; God has done it all. The next step is that anything that I would do is out of gratitude to God. But if I don't do anything at all, or if I do just a little now and then, in the end, it won't matter: God is still pleased with me, and I will go to heaven.

THE NOMINAL CHRISTIAN MIND

A new spate of literature from the recent past attempts to understand the nominal passive Christian mind. While these kinds of people are not found in Scripture, they do exist. Most pastors can point them out. Attendance, giving patterns, what they spend their money on, and what they read, watch, and participate in are strong indicators, as are the lack of personal evangelism and opinions on important social and cultural issues. Some of those we refer to as nominal passive Christians may not be Christians at all, or else they are poorly taught in the life of Christ. Whoever they are, they are a drag on the church and its mission.

One couple spoke of their membership in the same kind of church my wife and I attend. They had been longtime members, and their children had been baptized there. But they don't attend much anymore. Our conversation went into deep waters—cultural issues came up: politics, immigration, abortion, and the authority of Scripture. As we talked, it became apparent that the couple had a very different viewpoint from us on all these subjects. They had adopted a secular worldview that saw morality as a communal consensus rather than an objective, discernible system of truth. They had embraced identity politics as the best way to categorize people. It became apparent that they were ignorant of Scripture, so their life philosophy had been cobbled together from their cocktail circuit. Their guiding principle seemed to be whatever their friends and colleagues found acceptable.

Were these people Christians? They had believed in Jesus

Christ and that their sins were forgiven and that they were in good stead with God. They checked all the boxes of a plan of salvation, but their lives exhibited no evidence that God had shaped their identity or worldview whatsoever.

The late Christian philosopher Dallas Willard wrote about the passivity injected into grace:

> Salvation is free, which means you need do nothing else but "Accept." Then you too can sing Amazing Grace. Just observe who sings "Amazing Grace" now, and in what circumstances. You don't really even have to accept it, just sing about it. Not even that. It is wholly passive.[3]

This couple's entire religious story was based on a false premise. Someone had taught them that a profession of faith constituting belief and agreement with Christian dogma was what made you a Christian. Salvation was based on "grace," and so your status before God would never change, regardless of what you did, even if you walked away from your faith. So many have professed to be Christians, but they have nothing to show for it. Not a changed mind, a changed heart, changed behavior, or changed relationships. At some point, they drop out; they become what some call "done." They are done with the church; it is no longer relevant. But they maintain their "faith," because that is a separate thing from living, from life itself.

A good share of people hear the forgiveness-only gospel, get totally transformed, and begin a life of discipleship. Generally, they come out of a life that was so disgusting, so painful, that conversion washes them clean and sets them on a new course.

This happens mostly when a faithful friend is nearby to instruct them, to model the new life for them. Passivity doesn't occur to them.

Still, this leaves a church overwhelmingly populated with passive Christians. When one sees a catastrophe taking place, it is time to speak up. This is what Aleksandr Solzhenitsyn did when he wrote one of the most important books of the twentieth century, *The Gulag Archipelago*. As he exposed the hundreds of prison camps strung throughout the Soviet Union, Solzhenitsyn wrote and demonstrated that whole empires can be brought down if only one person stops lying.

The Danish writer Søren Kierkegaard was trained for pastoral ministry but never took up a pastoral role because of his insistence that the Danish church was corrupt. He was famous or infamous, depending on one's perspective, for his attack on Christianity. He maintained that he was not a Christian, even though he confessed to being in love with Jesus and true Christianity. Kierkegaard didn't want to be associated with the form of Christianity that the Danish church represented at that time. He spoke of his mission as introducing Christianity into Christendom. I am advocating introducing the gospel into our collective doctrine of salvation.

PASSIVITY VIOLATES COMMON SENSE

You can tell when something is just not true; common sense lets you know. For instance, we know that the intention to help someone is not as good as actually helping someone. The fact that Christians are concerned, moved, hurt, or inspired is of very little interest to God and to people who need help. Jesus' brother put it very well.

> What good is it, dear brothers and sisters, if you say
> you have faith but don't show it by your actions? Can
> that kind of faith save anyone? Suppose you see a
> brother or sister who has no food or clothing, and you
> say, "Good-bye and have a good day; stay warm and eat
> well"—but then you don't give that person any food or
> clothing. What good does that do?
>
> JAMES 2:14-16, NLT

His youngest disciple, John, put it this way:

> We know what real love is because Jesus gave up his
> life for us. So we also ought to give up our lives for our
> brothers and sisters. If someone has enough money to
> live well and sees a brother or sister in need but shows
> no compassion—how can God's love be in that person?
>
> 1 JOHN 3:16-17, NLT

Actions speak louder than words. Intention is essential, but actions are what can be witnessed. Actions mobilize intention and communicate love on a powerful gut level. A gospel of forgiveness alone, however, convinces us that our beliefs are more important than our actions. The plan of salvation approach to the Christian life devalues our actions almost entirely: No matter how good you are, the plan asks you to affirm that you can't work your way into heaven. Grace, we are led to believe, is diametrically opposed to works.

But God's grace is itself an action! If God related to us as though his actions had no inherent value, we would quickly consider him irrelevant to our lives. Perhaps this is why the watching world is indifferent, even hostile, toward Christianity? One of the most well-known verses in all of Scripture is "For God loved the world so much." If the verse stopped there, the world could retort, "So what?" God's love without God's actions is a cruel joke. The verse continues, however: "For God loved the world so much that he gave his only Son so that anyone who believes in him shall not perish but have eternal life" (John 3:16, TLB). The implication of the verse is Good News for all of humanity, but God's love requires God's action to mean anything. The only reason we listen to God is that he has acted.

WHAT IS TRUE?

It is important to say that the unbelieving community is not always right. In fact, there is reason to believe that they won't understand the Christian faith until they themselves become Christian (1 Corinthians 1:18-25; 2:14; 2 Corinthians 4:4). They are not always wrong, however, and they regularly attack us with our own stick. We point out the truth about sin, about the need to repent. They respond by confronting us with the teachings of Jesus. There have been many public embarrassments, clergy malpractices, molestations of young children, sexual excesses, big-name clergy defaming the name of Christ with financial scandals. They point out the clear contradiction between these scandals and what Jesus himself said and did. This is all shameful and causes us to hang our heads, but there is nothing quite as scandalous as the majority of Christians who passively skate through life behaving as religious consumers, who fit God in when they can. And the reason they do this? Because they think they can, because their leaders have told them they can, and because they think they will get away with it.

It should be said that no one ever gets away with anything, and we will be held accountable for every careless word we say and every deed we have done (Matthew 12:36; 25:29; Romans 2:6; 14:12; 2 Corinthians 5:10; James 4:17). Our careless words are the ones that reveal our darker nature. Christians are excused from hell—not from responsibility, not from accountability.

Paul worked to the point of exhaustion. He was focused and driven. He went through extraordinary hardships to fulfill his mission (Philippians 3:7-17; Colossians 1:28-30). Salvation is by grace alone, but grace that is truly grace and not mere self-delusion creates a life of discipleship. Sanctified passivity is the enemy of the gospel. May Jesus cast it out as the demon it has become.

THE GOSPEL OF THE LEFT PRODUCES ACCOMMODATION

To accommodate another person is generally considered good. You provided a service or a place to stay; you volunteered to give someone your bus seat; you did a good thing. Hardly anyone who accommodates understands their action as weakness; in fact, they see it as strength. But when it comes to your belief system, accommodating someone else's convictions at the expense of your own is an act of self-betrayal.

The worst part about accommodation at the level of conviction is that when someone is compromising, they usually don't know it. This happens at a very deep level, and rationalization is a major component. There are always forces at work in relationships, in the prevailing cultural norms, and, of course, in the mind of the one considering what to do.

Let's say, for example, that your scriptural position on human sexuality requires you to believe that sexual relations outside of marriage are always wrong, regardless of the form they take. But you have made friends with several people who are involved with others sexually outside of marriage, and it is considered quite normal to them. In fact, in your interaction with them, these relationships seem to be positive and doing no one any harm. You find yourself wanting to defend your friends and their lifestyles when other friends criticize such ways of life. You begin to reconsider your position; it seems like many of your more sexually active friends act more Christian and are better balanced than some of your uptight Christian friends. You think it might be time to take a second look at your scriptural understanding because so many Christians have now changed their view and their practices.

You begin to read an updated commentary on key texts that speak to sexual practices. You learn that many new discoveries illuminate our understanding of primitive Christianity. For example, young women were told not to engage in premarital sex because they were in their early teens and would be married by the time they were eighteen. That was a very wise guideline in ancient society, but now, women often wait for marriage until age thirty or later, and the idea of remaining a virgin for that long is unreasonable (and frankly, with birth control and modern medicine, not relevant). After a period of adjustment, you change your position, you change your practices, and you become an advocate of more freedom. This is how accommodation works. Your friends applaud you, and the church doesn't even know about it, as it is not something you announce to them. You become just another person who listens to sermons and believes a little less of what is said every Sunday.

THE MYTH OF HUMAN PROGRESS AND THE GOSPEL OF THE LEFT

What undergirds the tendency to accommodate is the attractiveness of living a more enlightened life. When Friedrich Nietzsche announced the death of God, he said that it was old news, and it was time to acknowledge it as fact. He famously said that the Enlightenment philosophers and theologians had killed God, showing him to be unnecessary. He added that there wasn't enough water to wash the blood off our hands.[4]

Fyodor Dostoevsky concluded that without God, anything is permitted.[5] Nietzsche said the problem with this idea was that humans would lose their basis for morality and would need to find a new one. He didn't think the human race was up to the task. The present-day moral confusion is a product of this effort; it has proven to be a bridge too far. The mind without God replaces a Christian worldview with nothing, at least nothing useful.

What the secular mind cannot grasp is that God created us with a conscience, an innate sense of right and wrong that resulted not from a mindless evolutionary process. Somehow, without direction or design, humans developed compassion and manners from nothing more than the desire to survive. Many make a case for civilized life by pointing out the best nation in the world is Norway, a country that left God and Christianity behind long ago. But Norway was civilized by Christianity before it began to secularize, and its citizens are still living on the positive residuals of Christian civilization. It's the impact of Christianity, not the embrace of atheism, that has kept the world's conscience alive.

The deeper a secular spirit sinks, the more the virtues of God's presence will wane. The richer a nation, the easier it is for it to happen—the process is accelerated. Not only is this true in Scandinavia but also in Western Europe and now the United States and other Anglo nations. Morality by consensus is the result, and if your starting point for morality is unknown, accommodation and compromise are all that one has. Right and wrong is then a social construct indeed.

Yes, there has been much progress regarding the technology of society. The gains in science, medicine, transportation, media, and communication have made life easier and less harrowing, in some ways. But humans have proven that even with these gains, we are better than ever at destroying those who get in the way of what we want. Nations now have the tools to slaughter their foes in greater numbers than ever before. The wars and conflicts of the twentieth century led to the deaths of well over 100 million people: some in world and regional wars, even more at the hands of dictators enforcing genocide of certain people groups in their own nations. No enlightenment will improve human nature.

CONFORMITY

One last comment about why accommodation is pervasive. We have already discussed how the influence of friends on one another leads to an accommodation of convictions that results in conformity. What is needed here is a word about image and the media. We come from different generations: I grew up watching television when it dominated the media and controlled the national image; Brandon started with television but was introduced to other media—video games, gadgets, and a wider variety of technologies—each of which shaped his image of life. The worldview Brandon learned from *Sesame Street* was much more diverse than what I got from *Captain Kangaroo*. My hero, the Lone Ranger, was not a complex figure; he didn't seem to share angst or have a special relationship with Tonto. The heroes of the 1980s and early 1990s were Indiana Jones, Ghostbusters, Macaulay Culkin, and Johnny Depp.

The way I dressed was shaped by my peers and what I saw in magazines and on television. You could say that I dressed preppy: khaki pants, Oxford shirts, madras shorts in the summer, and a seersucker sport coat or a blue blazer. And, of course, no socks. This is the way most of my male friends dressed during the high-school years. My class's social club for boys normalized a certain level of cursing, discussing exploits with the ladies, participation in sports, and attendance at the proper social functions. After I became a Christian, I began discussing my faith with my friends in the club, many of whom, it turned out, were Christian as well. They went to church regularly, participated in their church's youth ministry, and were led by their parents in regular family prayer. I asked them why they went along with the behavior of the group. The answer was obvious: peer pressure and the desire to belong, to be successful and popular.

We all understand peer pressure and its particular power over us during adolescence. But most of my friends who were serious Christians rediscovered their faith by their early twenties. Their belief systems brought them back. The danger of the gospel of the left is that its theology changes your belief system and burns the bridge behind you: There is no way to get back.

The best thing I can say about the liberal church is that it is a great place to win converts. If you sense a call, it is easy to find people there with a religious interest who could use a dose of the real thing. The gospel of the left, the one that deconstructs Scriptures and changes the story, creates a community of wishful thinking. Very few of the mainline liberal congregations are thriving; they are shrinking, churches are closing, and their former members are either done or have found harbor in another place. The liberal church is a product of the liberal seminary. The liberal seminary is a product of liberal theologians. Liberal theologians are a product of European philosophy and theology produced by what some call the Enlightenment. The Enlightenment is a period roughly starting with philosophers like John Locke, David Hume, Immanuel Kant, Georg Wilhelm Friedrich Hegel, theologians Friedrich Schleiermacher, Rudolf Bultmann, and many others who sought to use reason to sort out what was true about the Scriptures and what was false. What was left when they were done was the story of a great teacher who didn't perform miracles, who didn't rise from the dead, and who won't be coming back to rule the world, judge the nations, and establish his Kingdom. They proposed that the church should not promise people fantasy but instead give them a job, health care, and a free education. But a nonaccommodating gospel that holds to the historical tenets of the faith is a much stronger basis from which to help the world. Accommodation makes you weaker.

THE PROSPERITY GOSPEL AND ENTITLEMENT

The prosperity gospel breeds entitlement. Four in every ten churchgoing evangelicals are being taught the prosperity gospel.[6] While most prosperity teachers wouldn't say they are materialists, there is evidence that indeed they teach material success as the primary way you measure your spiritual value. For our purpose here, the prosperity gospel teaches:

1. To receive material blessings from God, I have to do something for God;
2. If I give more money to my church and charities, God will bless me in return; and
3. God wants me to prosper financially.

The underlying belief system is that God acts if you have enough faith to believe him. Prayer then becomes a tool to force God to act; you give him no choice. Creflo Dollar writes, "When we pray, believing that we have already received what we are praying, God has no choice but to make our prayers come to pass . . . it is the key to getting results as a Christian."[7] In reality, our prayers are dependent on God's will, and the results of our prayers are controlled by God's choices. A person's faith is only one component of any prayer.

Preachers of the prosperity gospel model these beliefs by their ornate living, even when the people in their care are living under hard circumstances. They see their ministry as demonstrating the greatness of God and showing that his favor sits on those who believe wholly in him. This is why you find prosperity megachurches in America where the pastor and his family actually own the church property; they are owners of that church business. They argue that they started it, so they are responsible to steward it because God has entrusted them with it. In these cases, entitlement is a badge of honor, but as a strategy for raising children and developing societal character, it is a curse. It is hard for a rich person to enter heaven, even harder for his or her children to grow up as responsible, nonentitled citizens (Matthew 19:23-24).

Hardly anyone wants their children to become what the prosperity gospel is designed to evoke in people. Entitled people turn off almost everyone else (except, perhaps, for similarly entitled people). Why, however, are we surprised? About forty years ago, the social engineers in Western culture decided to remove merit from much of our system. It began with some good ideas, like trying to help disadvantaged people. But then it was decided to move beyond equal opportunity and engineer equal results. Children, in particular, were victimized by this odious and disgusting ideology—in a simple sports competition, there were no more losers; everyone was now a winner. You would be rewarded for finishing last. Everyone is special, and everyone wins; goodies for all. Of course, this confused the children. A child might reason, *I finished last or second to last, and I got a trophy. Why are they giving me a trophy? I don't think I should get one. Why do I have this?*

This is only symptomatic of a deeper problem that removes incentive to work hard and compete. When you reach maturity, you find out that hardly anyone thinks you are special and gifted or that you should be given advancement in the company for doing little. You didn't work hard, you didn't need to suffer or pay your dues, and your mother isn't coming over to the office to make the boss give you a better grade like when you were in fifth grade. I enjoyed reading Dr. Jordan Peterson's bestselling book, *12 Rules for Life: An Antidote to Chaos*. Rule 5 is "Do not let your children do anything that makes you dislike them." What does one's gospel naturally lead to and produce? That is the question we are asking of every gospel that we scrutinize. Why would we want to sponsor a gospel that created disciples we didn't like, society didn't like, and God wouldn't like?

I am related to, vacation with, travel with, and work with many adherents to the prosperity gospel. I like them as much as I like any group of people. Their belief system only surfaces when they gather for worship, when they pray, when they are in trouble, and possibly when they shop. In their heart of hearts, most of them know their gospel of glitter and gold doesn't really work in their ordinary lives. They don't really expect to order God around like a heavenly waiter. The whole system collapses in on itself, under the weight of its own reality.

God made us rational beings. We are made in his image, and our minds match the way the world works. We are all common-sense realists: We know that hard work produces a better life than laziness. We know that taking a bath makes you more presentable than not bathing. So if a preacher tells you that if you bless him with a gift, you will actually end up healthier with more money and get promotions at work, naturally you have a built-in skepticism. You want to believe it is true, but you know down deep that it is wishful thinking, mere piffle. If you don't think you are one of the four in ten Christians who have been showered with prosperity piffle dust, then more than likely, that urge you feel to buy something means you are a material-ist anyway. That is because we are all well-discipled consumers.

CONSUMERISM AND ITS GOSPEL

It is common knowledge that our first natures are hardwired. We breathe automatically, we get hungry without trying, and thirst is common to every person, good or bad. We must consume to live. Our second nature, however, is composed of habits we choose. I fall asleep without thinking, but I eat a doughnut instead of a hard-boiled egg for breakfast because I choose to. A modern consumer orders a venti, decaf, soy, extra-hot latte without foam because they can, because they like it, not because they will die without it.

If you thought you could get your spiritual needs met without all the hassle of finding a church, getting to know people, and worse, being known by others, wouldn't you? This is the cultural trend: Part of the reason fewer people attend church, or get involved, is a survival technique. We have been taught to protect ourselves, we have personalized our religion, and we have realized that in our current system, spiritual content can be consumed hassle-free. An *ism* is a doctrine or theory that ends up being oppressive and discriminatory in attitude and belief. Add *-ism* to the end of a word—sex, age, race—and you've entered troubling territory. Most Westerners think of consumerism as largely benign, but the damage it does to our discipleship runs much deeper than our wallets.

THE BIRTH OF CONSUMERISM

You can't have consumerism without the soil in which it can grow. That soil is individualism. The root of individual dignity and importance is Genesis 1:26: "Let us make human beings in our image, to be like us" (NLT). Every human has rights that should not be violated. And every life is meaningful—this is a Christian idea.

But at the dawn of the Protestant Reformation, modern individualism found some soil in which to grow. Catholics said, "You get God's grace by joining the church." Protestants said,

"No, you get God's grace by going directly to God and putting your faith in him." Individual freedom was born.

Martin Luther went on to translate the Bible into German. Prior to this, the Bible was almost universally read and preached from in Latin, rarely or never in the language of the people. He wrote a new hymnal and developed new theological systems to provide people with a viable alternative to the Catholic church. But even as he and his contemporaries formed whole new churches, the idea that the church was incidental, not essential, to a relationship with God had taken root.

Then another idea came forth: Could we have a society in which everyone didn't have to belong to the same church? This was in evidence during the American Revolution and led to the separation of church and state. At some point, there was a transition: The rights of the community and the common good were replaced by the rights of the individual. The focus of American life post–World War II has been on attaining individual prosperity and pursuing the good life, largely assumed to mean material gains and the freedom to choose. It is not a surprise, therefore, that trained consumers would view the church as a source of religious goods and services. The operative question asked by religious consumers is: What can you do for me?

Technology has turbocharged individual freedom and isolation, whether it be the cell phone or the laptop. As stated earlier, people used to gain identity from a group or community. You looked outside yourself for confirmation of what you were thinking. The group collectively determined who you were in relation to them. Now, people look inside, and in spite of what your family, church, or friends say you are, you are what you say you are.

Consumerism boosted by individualism has become an absolute. This is where the consumer gospel is quite dangerous: It discounts God's truth and makes a god out of personal desire.

HOW THE CONSUMER GOSPEL
DECONSTRUCTS DISCIPLESHIP TO CHRIST

The most telling revelation of the consumer gospel and its conquering of the American church is the way church members come and go to church. Since the 1970s, American Christians have shopped for churches. At that time, denominations still mattered to people, and the churched population usually tried their own denomination's church when they moved to a new city. By the 1980s, that trend was replaced by a change in both consumer and the church itself. People started looking for a church that would "meet their needs." This was primary rather than secondary, and churches began to change their names from First Baptist Church to Sandy Creek Community Fellowship. The church was saying, "We hear you, folks. The number-one thing you want is to meet your family's needs, and it has become our priority—we are getting down to business here." This seems quite smart and largely harmless—right? Right, if it stopped there, but alas, it didn't. When you think your desires are paramount, remember that desires are satisfied only briefly, because desire takes, it doesn't give, and it always wants more.

Individualism breeds self-deification. When desire rules, it can't afford to be wrong. And when its sovereignty is challenged, it fights back. Let's say someone decides to attend your church and to get involved. They are even effusive in their praise of the pastor's preaching. They love the worship, and their children like the youth pastor. They tell others with great joy how they were praying for the Lord's choice for a church and he answered their conditions. Praise his name; he checked off every box.

Two years later, you sit in a meeting with this same family. They quiver with anger that you, the pastor, had the audacity to not allow their oldest son to be a leader in the youth ministry because he was caught smoking pot at school. They wanted this embarrassment held in confidence and are outraged that you told the youth pastor, who made the decision. They want you to ask their forgiveness and to fire the youth pastor. They have forgotten that their son's future is better if he publicly confesses to his fellow youth leaders and is restored through the redemptive youth community. The same family who desired a perfect church now want a perfect family reputation. It is their right, it is what God wants them to have as well, and you are out of God's will by getting in the way. They do the only thing their consumeristic, individualistic frame of mind permits them to do: They leave the church in protest, threatening a lawsuit.

AND MUCH MORE

The consumer gospel has led to various anomalies, like rich and richer Christians who tithe only 3 percent.[8] The attendance patterns of Christians are in such decline that the newest research indicates that it is somewhat miraculous that some congregations continue to operate. In the 1970s, faithful church attendance was over three Sundays a month; today it seems to have declined to 1.6 Sundays per month. For evangelicals, 58 percent go once a week; the remaining 42 percent attend on average about once a month.[9] The percentage of Christians who have shared their faith in the last year is also in slight decline: Around 50 percent claim to have had a spiritual conversation with a nonbeliever. Interestingly, the two groups that share their faith the most are low-income and high-income Christians, with a sharp decline in the middle class.[10] This is not all consumerism bolstered by individualism, because the world, the flesh, and the devil have always been hard at work. But it tells us exactly how Lucifer and his gang have been at work through changing the worldview of Christ followers.

Jesus asks us to go to church for others. Lucifer says, "No, you go to church to get your needs met, to learn to love yourself, and to experience the presence of God. You need to feel it, or God isn't there." And the beat goes on.

THE GOSPEL OF THE RIGHT PRODUCES A JUDGMENTAL SPIRIT

The final dimension of the broken gospel is what we call the gospel of the right. By "right," we mean a gospel that is primarily preoccupied with accuracy. Accuracy is important, but perfect accuracy is an illusion. Dallas Willard said it well: "We are not saved because we are right, we are right because we are saved."[11] Any biblically oriented gospel includes repentance of sins and belief in the Good News of following Christ. The gospel of the right wants more, however—a lot more. It not only wants your soul, it wants your opinions, your diversity of thought, your will, and your doubts. A tribe that preaches the gospel of the right requires that you adopt their entire system as the only one that really hangs together philosophically and answers all the questions.

You may be wondering who these confident people are and what school of theology they represent. Some of their members are lovely followers of Christ, men and women of godly character. John Wesley was very much opposed to the doctrine of divine election, which he railed against in some very strong language.[12] George Whitefield was strongly Reformed, yet he and Wesley maintained a close relationship. (The kinder and more Christian actor in the dispute was clearly Whitefield. While some would consider Wesley's theology more user-friendly and for the common man than Whitefield's Reformed theology, Whitefield's Christlikeness reflected very well on his beliefs.)[13]

That is the point here: There are various pockets, whether Wesleyan or Reformed, who believe that if you don't agree with them on every point, you are misled. And often, those who are sure they are correct are quite arrogant in their conduct and conversation with others. There is also a political element in this tribe. They insist on you being in political lockstep and that you adopt a similar worldview regarding the problems of society—and the solutions.

This comes with a theological swagger and a separation from other parts of the body of Christ. I once mentioned in a sermon that in an upcoming election, tens of thousands of Christians would go to the polls and vote for a candidate whom we wouldn't support. This caused an uproar. A special meeting was held for me to explain to baffled congregants how this could possibly be true. They were not satisfied by my explanation; some wrote me off as their pastor. It is this ignorance joined to arrogance that has fouled the air; the watching world gets a whiff and concludes, "Judgmental hypocrites." They are wrong, and they are right. They are wrong because the majority of Christians are neither judgmental nor hypocritical, and they are right in that enough of us are to pollute the atmosphere.

There is a good bit of research that indicates that the watching world considers conservative-minded Christians judgmental. The Barna Group found that 24 percent of UK citizens described the church as hypocritical, 23 percent as judgmental, 20 percent as antiscience, 9 percent as relevant, 7 percent as generous, 5 percent as assisting people with economic needs, and about 25 percent still called the church good for the community.[14] The numbers that are most concerning are not the 24 percent who think the church is hypocritical or judgmental; that has been the case for centuries. The figures that disturb are the mere 9 percent who consider it relevant and 5 percent who perceive the church helps with economic problems. It is not surprising, though, that the polled public had a much higher view of actual Christians they knew than the imaginary Christians on which they were asked to opine.

WHO IS IN AND WHO IS OUT

Rightness is a heavy burden to carry. Sometimes, those of this ilk go too far in their zeal to assess the religious status of others. It should be noted that Jesus instructed us on this matter through an experience with his disciples. John mentioned that the disciples had seen someone using Jesus' name to cast out demons and that they "told him to stop because he isn't in our group." Jesus went on to tell him, "Don't stop him! Anyone who is not against you is for you" (Luke 9:49-50, NLT). Swagger and obsession with the accuracy tribe are about who is in and who is out. Jesus demonstrated the same resistance to stark and final judgments in a later scene.

> [Jesus] sent messengers ahead to a Samaritan village
> to prepare for his arrival. But the people of the village
> did not welcome Jesus because he was on his way to
> Jerusalem. When James and John saw this, they said
> to Jesus, "Lord, should we call down fire from heaven to
> burn them up?" But Jesus turned and rebuked them.
> LUKE 9:52-55, NLT

Jesus nicknamed James and John "Sons of Thunder" (Mark 3:17, NLT). It is a normal human tendency to think that you are right and that anyone who disagrees should be treated with harshness—something severe, even death. There is something dark inside us that jumps for glee when our opponents fail: It removes the competition and confirms our rightness.

The parable that reveals our propensity to declare who is in with God and who is out is the parable of the wheat and the weeds. The idea is simple: Those who follow Christ are the wheat; those who do not are the weeds. For our purpose, it is Jesus' explanation of the parable that matters. The wheat and the weeds live so close to one another that attempting to pull the weeds would damage the wheat. God alone knows who is in and who is out, and only his angels are capable of dividing them. "The Son of Man will send his angels, and they will remove from his Kingdom everything that causes sin and all who do evil" (Matthew 13:41, NLT). The gospel of the right champions a preemptive separation mentality. At one time, the separation was social in nature: no dancing, using alcohol, attending films or the office Christmas party, wearing loud clothes, or even watching television or buying or selling on Sundays. As these prohibitions fell by the wayside, a new kind of separation developed. This separation was to not become friends with non-Christians because the association could do you harm. At the same time, however, each Christian is called to be a witness (Acts 1:8). There is a dilemma: You are called to reach those you live among like wheat is to weeds. You are not to become yoked to these people, bonded to them relationally or in other covenant relationships. The only option, then, is to preach and proclaim the gospel to them. Take them to a meeting where someone yells at them or where they are told they are out, and the only way to get in is to adhere to your message. This becomes very difficult to do when your paradigm does not allow for trusted relationships, conversations, and listening.

This is why the gospel of the right tends to not produce converts from anyone outside their group. There seems to be more satisfaction in getting it right and proving others wrong than in making new disciples who are taught to obey everything Christ commanded—especially that part about making disciples, making more disciples, and making disciples in every nation, while at the same time not forgetting about new disciples in your own church. A good question to ask someone of this ilk is, "In the last three years, how many new disciples have you made from people outside your church who are eighteen years or older?" Don't be surprised if the one answering the question starts to squirm.

THE DAMAGE DONE BY THE GOSPEL AMERICANA

The Gospel Americana has created many passive, accommodating Christians who possess a sense of entitlement. They are trained consumers with a strong sense of individualism that overpowers the common good. A vocal minority are rigid and focus more on dogma than on making disciples.

The Gospel Americana has created even more people who have been told that they are Christians but who are not. Having churches populated with people who believe they are believers but aren't explains why so few professing Christians read the Bible, pray, give money, give time, or engage in any kind of mission. Why is it possible for people to believe they are Christians when they are not Christians? It is quite simple: They have been taught that to profess Christ is to believe in Christ is to follow Christ. They have been taught that belief and verbally professing agreement with doctrine is saving faith—it is not, it never has been, and it never will be. In this paradigm, conversion is necessary, discipleship is optional.

Fifty-one percent of Christians have not heard of the great commission.[15] Research has demonstrated that the younger the churchgoer is, the less likely they can identify the proper passage or explain what the great commission is or means. Again, we can trace the root cause back to bad leadership and even further back to unfocused graduate-school curriculum. This is a fascinating, tragic debacle because it has led to so many problems. We could go on concerning this (and we will in future chapters), but for now, what can be done?

Christians should stop asking, *How am I doing?*, and pastors should stop asking one another, "How is your church doing?" These are the wrong questions. They only enable our preoccupation with the wrong things. Jesus tells us to ask a different question: *How am I doing loving the people God has given me to love?* We are Christ's disciples—let's act like it!

We are encouraged to see growing dissatisfaction with the

Gospel Americana; our hope is that *The Cost of Cheap Grace* can point the way and inspire the imagination to replace it with a more biblical understanding of salvation. Let us start with putting aside our selfish ways, with taking up our crosses and following Jesus. That is the kind of life he has called us to, not the self-preoccupation that our society teaches us that is eating the heart out of the church. Let us reject the Gospel Americana and pursue the kind of life Jesus modeled for us.

EVERYTHING IS A TYPE OF PRAYER

The contemplatives tell us to close our eyes and find the place
    beyond words
Where prayer holds back the stream of mind,
Even if it only slows our we-think-we-understand-thinking down
    a bit, like a sheet holding back a wave of water, that's
    something still

It helps to hold your breath, too,
And to slowly notice how your breathing goes, like balloons falling
    into the sky
Because God is always breathing in God's self, beyond the aching
    hows and whys
God is always there, breathing rest
God Himself always sighing

Breathe it all in, then,
The mystery
And now your body can taste it, before your mind:
Every book, every poem and song, strong and standing in the sun
Which is the breath of God holding the same energy

God always aware of everything
Ever in joy and sorrow
Always ever crucified, always resurrected

I feel even in this moment of writing, all this wonder, bright
*   and sad,*
Like I felt the cold air in Maine
When the heat could barely muster itself against the coming winter
And there was nothing more beautiful than the brutality all
*   around us*
As the autumn stood still in its crisp burning, like a woman
*   blazing at the height of beauty*
With no fear of wrinkles or of grave to come, welcoming all into her
*   holy hands*
Welcoming all the stars that are held by God like tender hearts
These tender hearts engraved with never-ending hope

4

A NATION OF HERETICS

*America's problem isn't too much religion, or too little of it.
It's bad religion: the slow-motion collapse of traditional
Christianity and the rise of a variety of destructive
pseudo-Christianities in its place. . . .
. . . For all its piety and fervor, today's United States needs to be
recognized for what it really is: not a Christian country,
but a nation of heretics.*

ROSS DOUTHAT, BAD RELIGION

BILL

THE CULTURE IN WHICH WE LIVE is pluralistic. Heterodoxy has emerged as king. We are a nation of heretics.

The origin of *heresy* is *hairesis*—"choosing for oneself."[1] Heretics have always been in the minority. In earlier times and in culturally monolithic places such as Saudi Arabia today, it is rare to have someone depart from societal orthodoxy. In America, however, choosing one's philosophy, worldview, or designer religion is common, even expected.

Christian leaders and writers often complain about the growing pluralism in the culture, the loss of the Christian mind, and the collapse of cultural consensus on what is true. More of us are writing disappointment books about what has gone wrong. But we should recognize that absolute truth was not something that existed in the first century. The religious and philosophical pluralism that is present in the twenty-first century was present in the first century—and yet, the early church thrived, grew, and eventually dominated much of the world.

All is not lost then, is it? We can't re-create the first century. We can't even copy much of what the early church did because it can't be replicated. We are different, the culture is different, our education is different, our worldviews are radically different, and the way we live is not even close.

And yet there is plenty of reason to believe that God can have his way with a nation of heretics. But these heretics are not your typical burn-them-at-the-stake types. Most are not dancing before golden calves or spreading chicken blood on their neighbor's lawn. In fact, many of these heretics would call themselves Christians. Of course they believe in Christ, or in some manifestation of the "Christ" spirit. They claim to love

Jesus; they just don't go to church, or they have found a no-rules, no-hassle Jesus they like a lot better.

When missionary statesman Lesslie Newbigin returned to the United Kingdom after thirty-three years in India, he found a homeland that had been secularized during his absence. It was a different world from the one where Charles Darwin waited twenty years to publish *On the Origin of Species* for fear of the damage it could do to the Church of England.[2] A society where even Darwin considered becoming a clergyman, and all his colleagues still signed the thirty-nine articles of faith required of every faculty member and student at Cambridge. It didn't take Newbigin long to conclude that Western culture had become more resistant to Christianity than ever. He used the word *nihilism* to describe the underlying problem.

Nihilism comes from the Latin word *nihil*, which means "nothing."[3] This belief says that there is no such thing as absolute truth, that one cannot know if something is true or false, good or bad. The only thing left is the human will, the will to power, what philosopher Friedrich Nietzsche called *ubermensch*, the superman.[4] This evolutionary ideology provided some important groundwork for what later became fascism's master-race doctrine. What nihilism had replaced was belief in divine revelation, which had been shoved out of the public conversation. The only absolute truth was to be found in science.

CAN THE WEST BE CONVERTED?

Newbigin delivered a series of lectures at Princeton Theological Seminary in 1984, which were published as the book *Foolishness to the Greeks* in 1986. Three years later, he published *The Gospel in a Pluralist Society*. These two works remain vital to the contemporary understanding of what is required of the church to establish a missionary presence in a secularized culture. What Newbigin concluded was that the underlying nihilism of contemporary Western culture created moral confusion, despair, and skepticism. It encouraged everyone to seek their own truth, to design their own identity, to cut their own path through life; it created societies of heretics, people flinging themselves into life directed only by an ambiguous inner voice.

This has led to what Tim Keller has called the four narratives of advanced Western secularism (as mentioned in chapter 2):

- *the Identity narrative*: You've got to be true to yourself;
- *the Freedom narrative*: You should be free to live any way you want, as long as you're not harming anyone;
- *the Happiness narrative*: You should do what makes you happy, because the point of life is to enjoy it; and
- *the Morality narrative*: No one has the right to tell anyone what is right or wrong for him or her.

How do Christians break the news to the culture that these commonly accepted narratives are deeply contrary to the teachings of Jesus? Newbigin tells us three things a missionary encounter is not and then three characteristics that it is.[5]

A MISSIONARY ENCOUNTER IS NOT WITHDRAWAL

I grew up Pilgrim Holiness—Amish with electricity. We didn't go to movies, shop on Sundays, dance, smoke, drink, or go to parties. Our women wore no makeup or jewelry, including wedding rings; neither did they cut their hair or wear anything but dresses. Often, boys and girls were not permitted to wear normal gym clothes that bared limbs or that would reveal the female form. It could be said that the Pilgrims were not establishing a missionary encounter with the 1950s culture, but then again, they weren't trying. They considered being distinctive and separate as their Christian witness. Of course, this has changed dramatically in the last sixty years, and present-day Pilgrims, now called Wesleyans, are doing as well as most in attempting to reach their culture.

It can be fairly said that in the last half of the twentieth century, the evangelical wing of the church worked very hard attempting to penetrate the unbelieving population. It would also be fair to say that evangelicals held their own in church attendance and made great strides in social justice and com-passion ministry. Progressive Christianity, however, has suffered greatly in loss of members and funding. Research demonstrates that whatever they are doing, it isn't working—people aren't buy-ing it. Barna Global found that in the United Kingdom, only 33 percent of people surveyed thought the church was beneficial to the world. Those surveyed also thought the church should stick to weddings, funerals, and helping the elderly and poor. The survey collectedly kicked the church to the curb.[6]

Evangelicals have been aggressive and done a lot of good, but they have largely talked at the culture rather than engag-ing skeptical unbelievers or disappointed, nonparticipating believers. We have banged on the door of secular city, we have bulldozed our way into their field of hearing, but they are indif-ferent; they are not listening. This is because of the vast differ-ence in worldview.

My worldview begins this way: "In the beginning God cre-ated the heavens and the earth" (Genesis 1:1). Everything I believe starts there, and all the pieces of my understanding fit the premise. God made me in his image. He gave me a mind that looks at creation and says, "God, you exist" (Romans 1:18-21). The world makes sense because God gave me a brain that fits the system. I can see his invisible attributes, his eternal power, and his divine nature. I started life believing in God. He has to exist—it's all around me.

My next-door neighbor is a Buddhist. He meditates in the lotus position on his front porch, he burns incense, and he has statues of the Buddha. He has a very different worldview than me. For me to establish a missionary encounter with him, it will take more than just telling him what I believe because he doesn't have a place in his worldview for my belief system. He has assigned it some compartment in his thinking.

This is what James Sire meant in his book *The Universe Next Door*.[7] My neighbor lives just a few feet from me, but he resides in a different universe. I must take a trip, a journey into what it is like to live in his head, and then begin a conversation with him based on his worldview. So as Newbigin is telling us, I can't withdraw and just lob pithy sayings over to him on his porch.

Only three basic stories attempt to explain the world:

- *the Theistic Story*: A personal God began and sustains the world;
- *the Mystical Story*: The world is like an ocean, each of us is a drop of water, and collectively, we are God. Meditation and enlightenment are the means to experiencing that reality; and
- *the Secular Story*: The universe is a product of mindless, blind, evolutionary process. The origins, purposes, and meaning of such a process are unknown.

One of my favorite authors, Nancy Pearcey, makes the point that every philosophy has a worldview and a similar narrative.[8] Pearcey recommends that each philosophy must run the gantlet of the three questions that are most relevant.

- Creation—How did it start?
- Fall—What went wrong?
- Redemption—What can be done about it?[9]

Everyone has rationalization for their behavior. Ask questions and engage—it's a great place to begin.

A MISSIONARY ENCOUNTER IS NOT A TAKE-OVER

Simple observation of religion's history of take-overs should chase away any straight-thinking person from such an idea.

Every time a religious group has attempted to take over an entire society, disaster has been close behind. This has nothing to do with the truthfulness of religion. It has to do with forcing conformity, whether it's to Sharia law or some rehashed Israelite civil or ceremonial law extracted from the Hebrew Bible. Roman paganism with its forced homage to Caesar and Christendom with its kings, priests, and holy armies have proved bad for the state and even worse for the religion. Buddhist and Hindu tyranny is evident in China, India, Nepal, and Tibet.[10] Finally, secular philosophies that deny human freedom and violate basic human nature have led to great suffering, high body counts, and failure. Countries such as China, Russia, North Korea, and Cambodia have proven that ideologies typically enslave people and only prosper the elite. The rule of thumb is, *Don't try to do what God alone can accomplish.*

I recall the sobering statement from Isaiah that voices the words of Christ at his second coming.

Who is this who comes from Edom,
    from the city of Bozrah,
    with his clothing stained red?
Who is this in royal robes,
    marching in his great strength?

"It is I, the LORD, announcing your salvation!
It is I, the LORD, who has power to save!"

Why are your clothes so red,
    as if you have been treading out grapes?

"I have been treading the winepress alone;
    no one was there to help me.
In my anger I have trampled my enemies
    as if they were grapes.
In my fury I have trampled my foes.
    Their blood has stained my clothes.
For the time has come for me to avenge my people,
    to ransom them from their oppressors.
I was amazed to see that no one intervened
    to help the oppressed.
So I myself stepped in to save them with my strong arm,
    and my wrath sustained me.
I crushed the nations in my anger
    and made them stagger and fall to the ground,
    spilling their blood upon the earth."

ISAIAH 63:1-6, NLT

God is not indifferent about his creation; he is committed to smash, judge, and eliminate those dedicated to its destruction. That is his work alone, and it is his right alone. Our role is not to take over; it is to find ways to preach the Good News of the Kingdom to every people group in the world.

A MISSIONARY ENCOUNTER IS NOT AN ASSIMILATION

Our argument must change from "Christians aren't perfect, just forgiven" to "Christians aren't perfect, but we are giving it a go." We shouldn't be talking about salt and light unless we have something to offer. Again, if our message is that we can have our sins forgiven and go to heaven, but on earth, we don't have a better life or do any better than anyone else, then the culture laughs. I am afraid what has taken place is that the media has so ridiculed those who are distinctively Christian, those who have not assimilated, that the majority of Christians choose to disappear into the culture.

The unbelieving, watching world doesn't draw a distinction between Catholics and Baptists, or progressives and fundamentalists, or prosperity preachers and snake handlers.

Lesslie Newbigin saw this thirty years ago, when he wrote, "A church which is merely trying to keep up-to-date is much more pathetic and ridiculous than a church which is merely clinging to the past."[11] One thing the church can do is stick to the eternal aspects of truth. It has been said that if one is to marry the spirit of the age, they soon will become a widower. *Jesus is Lord* is true truth, it is public truth, and it is eternal truth—for all cultures. I recently heard a new rendition of Jesus' words at a nationally televised funeral. Jesus' words "I am the resurrection and the life" (John 11:25, NLT) were proclaimed as "I am resurrection and life." Take out the definite articles and you take out the actual resurrection and the actual life. The uniqueness of Jesus and the hope he provides have been assimilated into the deadly tissue of political and philosophical correctness. No one that the society cares about is offended, and no one is helped.

So far, we've addressed what a missionary encounter is not. Now, we must consider what it is.[12]

CONFRONTATION

Can you imagine walking into a room and simply stating straight Christian claims? It would create a furor: Some would scoff, others protest, and some would even feel sorry for you. Then there would be the accusations that you are on the wrong side of history, living in the past. There is confrontation because you are setting out to overturn the world's most fundamental beliefs. Whenever this has happened in history, depending on the time and place and the weapons possessed by opponents, Christians have been labeled, ignored, persecuted, or killed. How can confrontation be avoided? The only way to avoid it is to be indifferent to the needs around us. It would be to slip quietly into the culture and hide from Christ's call to take up our cross daily. You can't be a Christian—a faithful Christian, a truthful Christian—and not have confrontation, rejection, and even suffering. If there is no pushback, then either you have withdrawn or you are so hostile that people simply move away from you.

What kind of person is required to establish a missionary culture?

Paul was waiting in Athens for Silas and Timothy to join him. This indicates that Paul was both a proactive strategist and a passionate reactor to what was around him. Paul wasn't idle; he reasoned in the synagogue with the Jews and God-fearing Greeks and went to the marketplace every day. He didn't just go there, he spoke there. The reason Paul didn't just hang around the city and see the sights separates him from many of us. When contemporary Christians go to Athens and wait for our companions, we put on our tourist hats and see some of the greatest architectural sites and works of art in the world. We often do this for a few days before, after, or in the middle of a larger mission we have raised funds for under the guise of world mission. This is commonly known as a *missiocation*. We turn off the mission and turn on the tourist. Paul was not able to separate one from the other. The biblical text explains why: "While Paul was waiting for them in Athens, he was *deeply troubled* by all the idols he saw everywhere in the city." Something happened inside of him and caused him to act. "He went to the synagogue to reason with the Jews and the God-fearing Gentiles, and he spoke daily in the public square to all who happened to be there" (Acts 17:16-17, NLT, emphasis added).

When you become a follower of Jesus and are taught by Jesus, you see the world differently; you take on an entirely new worldview. You see what you didn't used to see. Before his conversion, Paul would have been troubled by the idols, but for very different reasons. He would have been outraged by the blasphemy, and he would have wanted to rebuke, punish, imprison, and execute all violators. But now that he had been transformed by grace, what he saw broke his heart. Paul's faith was deeply personal, but it was not private[13]—he had to speak.

The agora was much more than a place to buy food. Athens was the cultural center of the world. Its history is known to most educated people as the home of Socrates, Plato, and Aristotle. It was a cultural center with temples, courts, libraries, theaters, gymnasiums, and galleries. It is where you went to buy goods, do business, and settle disputes. There was no technology, no stock market, and no newspapers or journals. If you wanted to debate, you did that in person. If you needed to make a deal, you made it there. If you wanted to meet friends and relax, there were places to sit and talk.

Paul's reaction was caused by the many idols. Athens was a pagan society. Everyone had a favorite god, one for their region, town, or interest. There was a god for fishing, one for sex, one for art, one for the stars, and one for the many Greek gods from mythology.

The two English words *deeply troubled* are from the Greek *paroxysmus*, which literally means seizure. It also means to be angry, and from the exegetical realm, we can conclude it means to be provoked from something outside of yourself and to stay provoked.[14] Paul was not just troubled and the anger subsided; he was provoked enough by the idols that he went into the market-place every day to battle with Jews, God-fearing Gentiles, and the Epicurean and Stoic philosophers. And he didn't hold back: He went forward with Jesus and resurrection. There was a great deal of pushback: "What's this babbler trying to say with these strange ideas he's picked up?" (Acts 17:18, NLT). Paul ended up at the high council of the city. They invited him to present his ideas on Mars Hill, a special forum where new ideas were entertained.

You can't stay mad day after day and be engaging and interesting. Hostility wears out your welcome very quickly. But in this case, Paul was invited to a place of honor because he found a way to connect with the philosophers.

The actual emotion Paul was experiencing was more what God himself is recorded as feeling when he was called a jealous God. When a man and woman are in love, sometimes one or the other becomes jealous when another person shows interest in the person they care about. It is a compliment to the person you love that you become angry and even act a little weird in defense of your relationship. God cares about us so much that he is jealous for us. This same word *paroxysmus*, translated "deeply troubled," is used of God in the Septuagint to describe how he feels when he sees people worshiping idols. This is a healthy jealousy. God is angry because he wants the best for us, because he loves us so much.[15]

A missionary encounter requires both indignation and compassion. As Keller notes, "On the one hand, you can see the compassion . . . what did [Paul] do out there in the marketplace? . . . It says he reasoned, he dialoged. And he did such a good job, actually, that he was invited to talk . . . [to] the culture brokers."[16] This is why we mentioned earlier that the key to engagement in the post-Christian, post-truth world is to enter into the other person's worldview and critique from the inside. Understand their questions, ask your own questions, and establish a conversation. What are their idols, what is it they believe that would make their lives not worth living if they lost it? If you can answer that question, you know their idols.

CONVERTS

We now find Paul on the Areopagus giving one of the greatest sermons ever. This is the first time we hear the gospel totally outside of the Jewish context. It is presented with his hearers in mind. He doesn't bother them with questions they are not asking and history they do not understand. Their idols are new ideas—in fact, just about any novel idea. They worship intellect and reason: They are so proud of their cultural heritage dating back three hundred years that they have shrines and altars celebrating it. Paul points out their altar to the "Unknown God." They are proud of not knowing; skepticism is intellectually prized, and it's a sign of sophistication to be uncertain about things transcendent. Paul's expertise—which can only be attributed to a keen intellect, excellent training, the teaching of Jesus, and the Holy Spirit—makes a statement that cannot be ignored. "This God, whom you worship without knowing, is the one I'm telling you about" (Acts 17:23, NLT). A man of certainty in a land of uncertainty, among a group of skeptics for which certainty could be career ending, makes his case.

"He is the God who made the world and everything in it" (Acts 17:24, NLT). Paul immediately answers Nancy Pearcey's most basic human question, "What is this thing called life, and who started it—where did the world come from?" He goes on to tell them that this God is nothing like the capricious, selfish, vengeful gods they have given themselves to, whose shrines and altars surround them in everyday life. "Cruel and fickle, passionate and vindictive, jealous and insecure, petty and insane: the inhabitants of Mount Olympus represent an attempt by the ancient Greeks to explain the chaos of the universe."[17] This God who created everything not only has no needs and was not made with human hands but also decided who would live, when they would live, and where they would live. By the time Paul finishes, he has answered every major philosophical question asked by humans. He explains human beings' reason for existence, where we come from, and what can satisfy the longing every person feels.

> His purpose was for the nations to seek after God and perhaps feel their way toward him and find him—though he is not far from any one of us. For in him we live and move and exist. As some of your own poets have said, "We are his offspring."
>
> ACTS 17:27-28, NLT

This is a nonreligious way of explaining what life is for. Knowing what things are for is essential. All of existence is tied together with its Creator. No one can find the "sweet spot" without God. He brings it home with clarity and action points. Not everyone is a skeptic; in fact, most people want to believe in something transcendent. We are made to worship something bigger and better than ourselves. Lesslie Newbigin helps us here with some real basic thinking:

> What is obvious is that in all knowing, both faith and doubt are involved. We cannot begin to know anything except by believing something. To put it on the other way around: If we doubt everything, we will never know anything . . . you cannot begin by doubting. . . . Faith is primary and doubt is secondary.[18]

Honesty requires that we admit how little we know, how fragile we are, how little power we have to change the world, or even ourselves. And finally, how fearful we are of nonexistence, because we are made for life, not death. Death is an unnatural state; it is unknown to the living. God has stamped eternity on our hearts—it is built-in. That is what Paul has tapped into; that is why we exist and why we don't want to stop existing (Ecclesiastes 3:11).

> God overlooked people's ignorance about these things
> in earlier times, but now he commands everyone
> everywhere to repent of their sins and turn to him. For
> he has set a day for judging the world with justice by
> the man he has appointed, and he proved to everyone
> who this is by raising him from the dead.
>
> ACTS 17:30-31, NLT

You will notice how Paul enters their frame of reference and critiques their worldview based on their idea of truth. He doesn't try to hammer home a covenantal Jewish gospel about the promises to Israel bolstered by quotes from the Law and the Prophets. He just picks their worldview apart piece by piece by answering all the questions they spend their time discussing. They thought they were going to get another interesting idea they could reject. Another idea they could weigh and discard with the power of their intellect. Another novel idea that would fall short and that they would spend the day laughing at in prideful delight. He explodes their thought world with resurrection, an objective historical event. As soon as he is done, a missionary encounter is established because Paul gets the two signs of success, pushback and converts.

> When they heard Paul speak about the resurrection of
> the dead, some laughed in contempt, but others said,
> "We want to hear more about this later." That ended
> Paul's discussion with them, but some joined him
> and became believers. Among them were Dionysius, a
> member of the council, a woman named Damaris, and
> others with them.
>
> ACTS 17:32-34, NLT

We don't want the conflict, and we don't want the contempt, but then we don't get the converts. So let's return to the question that naturally falls to us: What kind of person does it take to establish a missionary encounter with friends, associates, family, and the people we meet and influence? The answer is someone who has the same heart and motivations as the apostle Paul. He was able to mix it up with them, to identify their idols, and to shape the gospel to deconstruct their worldview. Another way to say it is have the heart to step into people's lives, to be Christ for them in their area of need. Then they will listen to you explain how Christ is relevant to you.

It is important that we all have what sociologist Peter Berger called a "plausibility structure" for the Christian faith. A plausibility structure is "generally acknowledged . . . acceptance of which is taken for granted without argument, and dissent from which is heresy."[19] Berger argued that this did not exist any longer in Western culture regarding the Christian faith. But he did say that a person could establish a plausibility structure for the Christian faith. In other words, among a nation of heretics, Christians could create space around their lives that makes it plausible that the Christian faith is true and that denying it is a logical heresy. The most common example was Mother Teresa and her Missionaries of Charity. There is a story about a group of Hindu militants who protested Mother Teresa and her work in a public building in Kolkata. Local leaders pressured the regional mayor (top elected official) to find out exactly what took place there. The official spent about an hour inside. When he emerged, the mob expected him to capitulate and expel the sisters from the premises. But the official basically said, "Yes, they are Catholics. They do pray for their patients. Yes, some people are converted to the Christian faith in their last moments on earth—that is true. But what those Christian women are doing in that building is so remarkable, so moving, that unless you are willing to go in there and do what they do, the sisters will remain." After hearing the official's statement, the protesters dispersed.[20]

Their viewpoint was not plausible, but Mother Teresa's was. There is nothing worse or more implausible than bad religion. Good religion still possesses the greatest plausibility for the truth of the Christian faith.

BEWARE OF EXCEPTIONAL EXAMPLES

Great examples often work against the reason a person has for using the example. Jesus is always the best example. We are told to be like Jesus, but we all know that we can't be Jesus, and even behaviorally, we can't duplicate his works. He says we can in John 14:12-14, but it is impossible to better the quality of Jesus' life and work. It is possible to exceed the works of Jesus, however, based on the context of John 14. Jesus was referring to what he had done on earth to that point, but his disciples would exceed him in spreading the gospel and in the number of people who would believe. Paul is also a great example that makes him the exception rather than the rule. Don't compare yourself to Jesus and Paul when it comes to brains, talent, grit, and courage. Examples are there to encourage us, to show us something important, not to discourage us because we can't measure up.

Bad religion has created a nation of heretics. Disciples, men and women of good witness whose lives and stories provide a plausibility structure that makes the gospel plausible to the general public, are the solution. The question is about what Paul was: How do we get there—see what he saw, feel what he felt, and do what he did?

The one thing to remember about Paul in Athens is to ask God for a heart that is both provoked and broken when you see people worshiping idols. Then you must put off old patterns of thought and practice and be willing to be among people who need God. Sometimes this is as simple as leaving your home, but for some, it will require making new friends, changing schedules, joining a club, learning a sport, or taking up a hobby. Find a place where people gather, people you could grow to love the way God has loved the world from the beginning. Then converse with them to learn their stories and understand their worldviews. Be willing to ask and answer questions and then just come out with the truth as Paul did. He used the word *resurrection,* and he claimed that Jesus was the truth not only in Jerusalem but also in Athens. He was the truth on the Damascus road, and he is the truth on Mars Hill and on the steps of the Acropolis. The Greeks spoke much of the Logos, the divine transcendent Word. Jesus was proclaimed as the Logos. God spoke to his creation in a living Word, in a person. Jesus was and is the most eloquent statement ever made. Please allow Lesslie Newbigin to help conclude the chapter:

> . . . the ultimate reality, the ultimate secret of eternal truth, for which the Greeks gave many names but one of them was the name Logos, the Word, the reason which ultimately, beyond history, is the locus of reliable truth. That this Word has become flesh in the man Jesus Christ, whose ministry, death, and resurrection is the manifestation of God's eternal being. . . . The ultimate reality is no longer something available to reason and to the mind of the philosopher. It is to be known by accepting and following the call of Jesus, that the answer to the question *What is the ultimate secret of the universe?* is this man Jesus.[21]

Yes, the West can be converted if we confront, have converts, and start knocking down the idols, starting with our own.

I TRUST THE CRUCIFIED GOD

I saw God in a back room, bound and gagged
Looking out, at once, on everything,
Weeping
Lamenting all there is to hold
And all that we let go of
And all that's pulled from us
In this cruel world

Then the door was shut and
What business was conducted
I'll never know

I'd seen him in the afternoon
His nose pressed up to the Metro window
Taking it all in:
The great caressing beauty of it
The soul crushing ugly of it
The stink that makes you quake
The heart shaking in fits of rage
At all the desire it can't rein in

I trust the crucified God from whom the universe unfurled
Who knew that insecurity and doubt and suffering would become
*   the only air for lungs to breathe, like gas filling the great*
*   vacuum of us,*
For any form of life to take—
Every space, for good and evil, must be filled
Every possibility penciled in

He knew all this

Knew it would be villainy atop the towers
And in the streets
And at our feet
Rose petals among the excrement
As we sit with our pierced longing,
As we bleed from wounded sides

I will trust and honor
Any God who so surrenders
Any God who,
In His creating, Himself is pained
And finds Himself hanging, already crucified
Held by Love
Prefiguring in His already pierced person
All that was to come

5

RETURNING TO THE BIBLICAL GOSPEL

*One has to start with what you preach
as the message of salvation.*

DALLAS WILLARD

BRANDON

PEOPLE HAVE BEEN TRAINED TO THINK that "having faith" means simply "believing that God can and will forgive your sins." Having faith, of this sort, satisfies the religious requirement, so why would we move on into discipleship? And even when people have a desire for discipleship, the shadow of the nondiscipleship gospel often obscures the path they might take. So much time has been spent on "getting souls into heaven" that even those desiring discipleship might not easily find a soul-transforming discipleship path.

As we've previously discussed, this narrow understanding of faith as "believing that God can and will forgive your sins" is a consequence of the Gospel Americana, a slow-cooked erosion of the gospel that came about as the correctives of the Reformation commingled with the reductionist thinking and cultural norms of the Enlightenment. Then, in an American society that sought quick-and-easy formulas to explain complex concepts, and an increasingly consumer society at that, the Good News of the gospel has gradually become a life of ease made possible by Christ, rather than a life fully surrendered to him. This Gospel Americana must be unlearned so that the true gospel can rise in its place.

Of course, it's hard for any of us to learn something when we think we already know it.[1] We must be willing to look more deeply at what we think we know. When we do, we are poised to expand our understanding.

Matthew Bates, for example, makes the potent argument that the word *pistis*, which in the New Testament is generally trans-lated as "faith" and/or "belief," had a more robust connotation in the first century. He writes, "The Greek word *pistis*, generally rendered 'faith' or 'belief,' as it pertains to Christian salvation, quite simply has little correlation with 'faith' or 'belief' as these words are generally understood and used in contemporary Christian culture, and much to do with *allegiance*."[2] In other words, to believe in (*pistis*) Jesus was not just to have faith in him but to be allegiant to him in every area of life, thereby being able to wholeheartedly declare, "Jesus is the King to whom I give my loyalty."[3]

The fear of language like *allegiance* is works theology, the heresy that by doing good work, we can earn our salvation. But the requirements of transformation described in Scripture are not burdensome because they are borne out of union with God, not just by our effort to work harder.[4] Jesus says this in precise terms: "I am the vine; you are the branches. . . . Apart from me you can do nothing" (John 15:5; cf. Matthew 11:29-30). The writer of Hebrews makes it clear that we do not labor to earn anything but rather we labor to rest in the provision of God's grace (Hebrews 4:11). Spiritual disciplines, as Dallas Willard so often taught, are not about our producing anything but rather about our willingness to let the life of God produce life in us. The "fruit of the Spirit," after all, is not "the fruit of our labors." But at the same time, our efforts are absolutely part of the process (and self-control, which is certainly a function of our will and discipline on some significant level, is also a fruit of the Spirit).

We focus on our union with God, which leads us to good works without legalism on the one hand or arrogance on the other. This union, always described in the New Testament through metaphors of forgiveness, adoption, and new life, must pour forth in a transformed life and transformed action for the sake of the world. This is not works righteousness; this is an understanding that adoption into the family of God means coming to look like God, as the New Testament makes absolutely clear (e.g., 2 Corinthians 3:18). New works are the fruit of transformation and are always the overflow of grace, which is part and parcel of new life in Jesus.[5]

Indeed, in Scripture, faith and works are in a tension, a paradox, a both/and held together by the saving work of Jesus on our behalf. Just as both grace and the faith to receive grace are gifts, so faith and its companion, works that testify of faith, are gifts. And both our faith and our works are proper responses to the gospel.[6] Paul (as Jesus did before him) makes it clear over and over again that we will be judged by our works, not because the works in any way save us but because the works go hand in hand with our faith in Jesus (Romans 2:6; see also Matthew 7:21-23; 25:31-46). Our work is to make present the Kingdom of God, not to go to heaven when we die. Faith and works are part of the same movement of allegiance to God which typified the understanding of the early Christians, under the motto "Jesus is Lord."

This way of understanding requires a new way of thinking. And it means we must return to the world of Hebraic thought, to the world of Scripture and of Jesus, if we want to escape the false dichotomies—between conversion and discipleship, between faith and works—of our day. Only then can we pursue discipleship freed from the emotional stuckness and the limited thinking that has so crippled the American church.[7]

REBUILDING THE DISCIPLESHIP GOSPEL: BIBLICAL PARADOX AND BOTH/AND THINKING

Mystery isn't something that is gradually evaporating.
It grows along with knowledge.

FLANNERY O'CONNOR

To understand Scripture and become a mature disciple, our minds must wrestle with paradox. Ultimately, this wrestling not only helps us become mature, it also helps us recapture what has been lost in the ancient understanding of the gospel. The contemporary gospel—the Gospel Americana—has often been obsessed with certainty and having all the answers. Information and answers are important, but they have limits; we are asked to trust Jesus as the Answer amid many uncertainties and in the midst of *not* having all the answers.

Scripture trains us toward this appreciation of mystery. It points to paradoxical realities: God is three but one. Jesus is human and divine. We are sinners, yet we are adopted and beloved children of God. Some paradoxes we simply accept as beautiful mysteries. Others we resist because we want a linear world that makes immediate sense. Theological wars have been fought over God's sovereignty versus human free will. In a chaotic world, we want answers, not paradox. We like either/ors that enable us to live in a tidy, stable world. How can God be sovereign and yet we have free will? What does that even mean? Even attempting to think in both/ands can hurt our brains. It's uncomfortable. But such both/ands serve to humble us. They teach us that we live in a beautiful, mysterious world, that we are very small, and that there is much that we do not fully grasp. This humility and the appreciation of mystery help us live awe-filled, hope-fueled, praise-centered lives as disciples of Jesus. We can appreciate the complexities of life, which point us toward gratitude and worship that God holds all of reality.

Nevertheless, this is difficult work. We live in a society that encourages us to think only in either/ors. You would think that, with the ascendance of postmodernism, we would have a higher tolerance for paradox, but oftentimes, the opposite holds true. The algorithms of Facebook ensure that we are presented with articles and links to stories that confirm our established point of view, so we can readily confirm our biases. And we are often given only simple options to complex problems. Take, as an example, the controversy over NFL players kneeling during the national anthem: The mainstream options given were to see those who kneeled as (a) righteous protestors of evil America or (b) America-hating ingrates. Choose a side. But was that situation really so simplistic? Isn't it possible, for example, to kneel during the national anthem not out of ingratitude but as a way of pointing out that America has further to go in living out its founding creeds? Isn't it possible to stand and sing during the national anthem while still protesting ongoing systemic injustices? Instead, "it's a completely polarized choice. Either they must stand and accept everything the anthem stands for, or sit and be perceived as rejecting one's country."[8] We don't get into the nuance; it's easier just to take sides and dismiss any troubling complexities. And public space to address these sorts of issues with any level of thoughtfulness and nuance are vanishingly rare. The twenty-four-hour news cycle has not only turned news into entertainment but also into echo chambers calibrated to niche demographics; people tune into Fox News or MSNBC and confirm whatever point of view they already hold.

Either/or thinking is often rife in our approach to God, too. Many people who genuinely seek a deeper relationship with God cannot reconcile God's holiness with his love, nor his transcendence ("out-there-ness") with his immanence ("right-here-ness"). So they see God as holy and distant (more than loving and near) and their spiritual life is, consequentially, flat. The trade-off is that they don't have to wrestle with the paradox that God is holy *and* loving, transcendent *and* immanent. That allows them to avoid the face of a close, loving God, so they escape the humility and vulnerability such a reality would demand. In fact, on some level, we prefer relating to God as cold and distant. We don't feel compelled to render our lives to such a God, which allows us to feel like we're in control. The root of mere religion is such thinking: *If I do things well enough, God will like me and give me a gold star. I can go through the motions without having to endure uncomfortable internal change.*[9]

A LONG HISTORY

Marvin Wilson helps explain why Westerners have such a hard time embracing biblical paradoxes.[10] We have been schooled, Wilson says, in the either/or syllogism of Greek thought. If *A is to B* and *A is to C*, then *B is to C*. And if a proposition is true, then its opposite is not true. This is all neat and tidy thinking, and helpful, as it does help us understand much of reality. But it is also limited thinking, with little room for mystery or paradox. It creates a stuck system of logic, and a stuck system inhibits new growth.

In Hebrew thought, there is far more capacity for accepting that both a proposition *and* its opposite might be true. We see this sort of nuanced thinking throughout Scripture. For example, in Proverbs 26:4, we are told *not* to answer a fool according to his folly (or we may become like him). In the very next verse, we are told *to* answer a fool according to his folly (or he may become arrogant). Both seemingly contradictory aphorisms are true, then, depending on the context.

Wilson calls the capacity to think in such terms, above linear thinking, "block logic." We hold two propositions in our hands which, on first look, seem contradictory and accept that they are both true, that they resolve in God somewhere beyond our understanding. Without such understanding, God, faith, and life become very frustrating as we try to resolve things that can only be held in tension.[11] How else can we deal with suffering but by knowing that *God is good* and yet *there is evil in God's world*?

Jesus appealed to paradox when discipling those who followed him. After all, how could Jesus be "Joseph's son" from Nazareth and also the Christ, who "came down from heaven"? (John 6:42, NTE). Jesus allowed his followers to hold and wrestle with this both/and. But Jesus also instructed his disciples to hold both/ands by how he taught them. When they came across a man blind since birth, the disciples asked Jesus, "Who sinned, this man or his parents, that he was born blind?" (John 9:2).[12] They wanted a tidy formula: This man was sick because either he sinned or his parents did. Such a karmic universe would give us a sense of control and a sense that we are good (we aren't sick, so we must be good people). The disciples might have been raised in a culture with greater appreciation for paradox, but the human longing for certainty is stronger than any culture.

Jesus responded by saying, "Neither this man nor his parents sinned, . . . but this happened so that the works of God might be displayed in him" (John 9:3). Honestly, what kind of answer is that? Well, for one, it was an answer that pushed them out of tidy either/or thinking (in this case, that suffering could always be explained by someone's bad behavior—either this man sinned or someone else did). Jesus asked them to hold the tension that, even in God's good world, there is suffering. But he pushed them through this both/and into a new way of thinking: Nevertheless, God would redeem even this suffering and be glorified.

The heart of either/or thinking is seeing only one side of an equation—one side of reality. For example, some sickness does come through sin (not taking care of your body, et cetera), so let's just say that *all* sickness does. Thus, at the heart of either/or thinking is a truth that is only half told and that does not fully reflect reality. The problem of evil and suffering is another example. If there is evil in God's good world, the problem must be with God: He is either unable (not powerful enough) or unwilling (not good enough) to deal with the evil. But accepting that God is good and powerful and yet there is evil in God's world forces us into new ways of thinking; God seems to have limited himself in this world, and yet, he comes to suffer with us—to be with us in and to bring us out of suffering.

In the mind, discipleship is first making space in our imaginations for paradox. The tension of paradox then shapes our hearts. Rather than reducing God to either unable or unwilling to address evil, we make space to realize—and ultimately experience—that God suffers evil with us in the process of overcoming it. And once we've reached that level of spiritual understanding, our ethic is transformed: We suffer with those who suffer and demand justice for those who suffer. You can see how both/and thinking changes how we live as disciples.

Indeed, both/and thinking is at the heart of spiritual maturity. When you can hold—not only in your mind but also in your heart—the reality that you are completely unworthy and yet completely worthy in God, you have moved into spiritual maturity. And when you can hold that God is holy and loving, you are moving into a mature view of God.

As we have seen, the Gospel Americana twists scriptural realities, doubling down on either/or thinking. We are saved by grace, and we are empowered to live faithful lives by grace, but in the Gospel Americana, one side of the equation—saved by grace—reigns supreme. The Gospel Americana takes both/ands and offers reductionist formulas: God is holy and kind, but God's holiness is irrelevant to us. The cheap grace gospel tells us that God's kindness has won the day. By the same token, it is easy to think that God is so loving that he couldn't possibly be chagrined by our bad behavior. He simply wants to make sure we feel okay about ourselves.[13] The call to right action and good deeds and the demand to make present the Kingdom of God—the entire story of the book of Acts, for example—is dismissed as immaterial.

The church *is* changing, thank God, but the influence of the Gospel Americana is a hard ship to turn. If we want to recover the gospel that Jesus taught, we must expand our capacity to think as Jesus did. Then we can resist the neat and tidy boxes of the Gospel Americana ("Pray the Jesus prayer, and you'll go to heaven when you die") and hold instead the tensions and paradoxes of discipleship.

With an acceptance of both/and thinking, we can approach discipleship with a renewed mind. We can embrace that we are saved by grace *and* transformed by it—and that we cannot have one without the other. Further, when we seek to make disciples, we will look to shape not only the mind but also the heart. In fact, like Jesus, we will encourage people to wrestle with paradox and all the tensions of life, so they have opportunities to grow in trust.

THE ULTIMATE BOTH/AND: CONNECTING MIND AND HEART

Not only did Jesus instruct his disciples to hold tension in their minds, but he connected their minds to their hearts. This connection between mind and heart is the ultimate both/and.

In a way, almost all the Judaism of Jesus' day was based on formula: Our ancestors didn't keep the law and were punished. We will keep the law and be rewarded. Whatever capacity for both/and thinking might be present in Hebraic thought, the human tendency to prefer formulas over paradox often wins out, in any culture. In our day, much of what we have called discipleship has been based on a contemporary formula: *information = transformation*. This formula allows discipleship to remain a matter of the head but not of the heart.

Consider how the formula *information = transformation* plays out. You go to a class at church and read some books on discipleship and, voilà, you're transformed. We think that confirmation of *information = transformation* of character. That's the implicit promise. But the point of paradox is that people must trust God with their hearts—even when not everything is sorted out in their minds, even when the world seems to make no sense at all.

The disciples can't immediately understand what Jesus means by "the glory of God" being revealed in the blind man, so they are left to wrestle. When we are in paradox or a wrestling tension, we can look to God, since we don't have the answers within our own selves. Jesus' formula for transformation, then, looks like this: *transformation = information + trust.* Jesus *does* give the disciples information and clear instruction. He explains to them what parables mean (e.g., Matthew 13:1-23). He teaches them how to pray (Matthew 6:9-13). But he generally follows the information he gives with a tangible lesson about trusting God in the midst of tension. Shortly after teaching the disciples to pray, he lets them sweat out the storm on the Sea of Galilee so they learn that faith requires real, not conceptual, trust. In fact, Jesus consistently *induces* tension. Before he miraculously feeds the five thousand, he says to his disciples, "*You* give them something to eat" (Mark 6:37, emphasis added). Their work as disciples is not just to learn about what he's doing but to do it themselves! We are only transformed when we are in the practice—not just the theory—of trusting God.

Indeed, Jesus takes the disciples to places where they can learn to trust. For example, he takes them to the most unclean place the purity-minded, orthodox-Jewish brains of his day could imagine: to a naked (that's one purity-code violation) demon-possessed (that's two) man living in a graveyard (three) next to a herd of pigs (four; Mark 5:1-20; Luke 8:26-39). He does this to put them in the tension of seeing that God's heart for the lost and hurting transcends their obsession with purity codes and who's in and who's out. But this is real tension they must navigate, not unlike Jesus sharing meals with sinners and tax collectors and talking to a Samaritan woman. We prefer the mental exercise. *This person is a Samaritan and those people are Gentiles; therefore, they are out. We are Jews; therefore, we are in.* Jesus will not allow his disciples to relate to Samaritans or Gentiles with a cold heart, nor will he allow us to relate to ourselves out of pride or vanity.

Discipleship is not a mental exercise (although within the Gospel Americana, that's exactly what it has so often been reduced to). With an acceptance that Jesus cares not just about our minds but our hearts, we can approach discipleship willing to embrace the tensions that are necessary for our transformation. Anyone seeking to grow in discipleship—or in disciple making—should look for places of conceptual tension and move toward them, asking God to help them trust him in the process. This was Jesus' way of making disciples. And it takes us far beyond the reach of the Gospel Americana.

Renewed thinking gets us on track. But to fully reclaim the discipleship gospel, we must attend to language and imagery. Specifically, we must embrace the language and metaphor of the Bible, which can free us from the grip of the Gospel Americana.

THE IMPORTANCE OF BIBLICAL LANGUAGE AND IMAGERY

Language is God's primary way of communicating with humans and humans' primary way to understand each other. Words are mere symbols that create images in our brains that make it possible for us to live together in relative harmony. "Please pass the butter," at least in most places, will get you butter. But the word *gospel*, or *Jesus*, or *disciple*, or *convert*, or *discipleship*, or *disciple maker* creates multiple pictures in our minds. Each one means different things to us based on our background. If the church (or just a local church) is going to make disciples who make disciples, the definition of a disciple must be clear.[14] Words, after all, can mean different things to different people.

In the first pages of this book, we discussed two different ways of understanding the word *salvation*. Broadly speaking, in the Gospel Americana, salvation means that you are saved from your sins and know you will go to heaven. In the understanding of Jesus and the early church, salvation meant something different:

> the process of God calling a person to a reconciling relationship, leading to repentance, forgiveness, new birth, and a life of following and learning from Jesus. This includes participating in his values and his mission. The culmination of this good life is stepping into the eternal state of an active life with him.[15]

These are two vastly different interpretations, and they lead to two very distinct practical outcomes: one in which people passively wait for heaven and one in which disciples give their lives to the work and mission of God in this world.

In Christian history, language has often been greatly abused or, at the very least, made impotent. Consider a simple—yet sobering—example: Is the work of the church the salvation of souls? This was the understanding of the conquistadors, who baptized "converts" en masse even as they raped and pillaged the same people. After all, as long as you save the soul, what does it matter what you to do the body or all of creation?

If, on the other hand, you understand salvation as the coming of the Kingdom of God—the renewal of all things, including not only souls but bodies and ultimately all of physical creation—you go about your work completely differently, and raping and pillaging are abominations.

Much has been written—thank God—on the need to move our theology away from "incanting anemic souls into heaven," as Wendell Berry so wonderfully put it, and the concurrent need to move souls into a vibrant life of scriptural transformation, to look like Jesus.[16] That, of course, is part of the aim of this very book. But we *do* believe our goal is to get souls into heaven. The problem, again, is one of language. Namely: What on earth do we mean by *heaven*? Use the word and many picture clouds in the skies on which souls—somehow embodied—are playing golden harps. It's the place we go when we die. But, as N. T. Wright has doggedly demonstrated, this is a fundamental misunderstanding of the narrative of Scripture. After all, the story is not primarily about our going to heaven but rather *heaven coming to earth*.[17]

Jesus defines heaven as "eternal life";[18] it's not primarily a place but a state of being. To have eternal life is to *know* God, in this world and the world to come, intimately, experientially, rather than just holding information in our brains (John 17:3). To live in eternal life, therefore, is to live wherever we are in a deep knowing of God that is not merely cerebral but is also emotional, psychological, spiritual, and even physical, alive in all our senses.

Heaven, then, is being in this state of ever-deepening union—always moving "further up and further in," as C. S. Lewis put it—both in this world and in the world to come.[19] It is a mistake to think that you will be instantly zapped into this alliance and eternalized in union with God if you never longed for that, let alone pursued it on this side of the grave.[20] Yet many people deeply believe, "I'm a Christian. I'm not going to hell when I die; I'm good."

Language is powerful, but when words come to represent something they were not meant to, we remain blind while thinking we see. Like old flooring that must be pulled up to make way for new flooring, you can only lay down the new foundation of salvation as participation in God's new life and heaven as union with God if you tear up the old foundation of salvation as going to heaven.

REBUILDING THE DISCIPLESHIP GOSPEL: RECOVERING THE BIBLICAL LANGUAGE OF DISCIPLESHIP

When we look at the vocabulary of discipleship in the context of Scripture, a powerful reclaiming of language that has all too often become watered down in our contemporary context can take place. Dallas Willard writes:

> The teaching about salvation that is now an American cultural artifact is that you confess faith in the death of Jesus on your behalf, and then you join up with a group that is trying to get others to do the same. That is all that is essential. So it is thought and taught. "Spiritual growth" is not required on this scheme, and there is no real provision for it.
>
> Salvation is free, which means you need do nothing else but "accept." Then you too can sing Amazing Grace. Just observe who sings "Amazing Grace" now, and in what circumstances. You don't really even have to accept it, just sing about it. Not even that. It is wholly passive.

To deal with this situation, one has to start with what you preach as the message of salvation and what you take salvation to be. Salvation is spiritual transformation, which is not an option for those with special interests. Grace is situated in that "salvation." If you had a group, and you wanted to see such salvation in them, you would have to start from the beginning and teach closely. Do inductive Bible study on "grace" and all of the other central terms of our church discourse, and build your preaching and teaching around what you discover. Remember to include "repentance" and "faith." You would probably lose a lot of people, and have to rebuild your work. . . . The earliest church is the best illustration of the painful process and of the success that can accompany it.[21]

Let's look at the biblical words Dallas directs us to examine.

SALVATION

We must not think of being saved as having a ticket to heaven but rather as being in a relationship that utterly transforms us. It strips away our ego, which can be painful to us, but it also always leads us into Resurrection life as we learn to live from the power of God's Spirit within us (cf. Romans 8, especially 14-17).

This full, scriptural sense of salvation sets us up for a transforming relationship with God that begins at conversion and continues into the world to come, rather than a mere transaction with God having the limited consequence of getting us into heaven. As if we could stand the glory of God in heaven while having no appetite for transformation while on earth![22]

FAITH

Faith is not just belief that God is good or trusting that he saves you from your sins, though it certainly includes those realities. It is also allegiance to God, demonstrated in action in everyday life. It's participation with God in God's work in the world. "Faith . . . is also faithfulness," as Scot McKnight says simply.[23]

We must not think of faith as something we have that gets us saved but rather as a response to God's own faithfulness to us.[24] It is binding ourselves to the one who saves us.

GRACE

In contemporary usage, grace is associated with forgiveness but not with new power for living. Dallas Willard once quipped, "We have not only been saved by grace, we have been paralyzed by it."[25] His point was simple: When grace is taught as a one-time dollop of God's favor that falls out of the sky on your unsuspecting head, saving you, Christians are left lacking further categories for thinking about grace, so they have little expectation of an empowered life.

In the biblical usage, grace is, as Dallas Willard summarizes, "God acting in our lives to bring about what we do not deserve and cannot accomplish on our own."[26] Ben Sobels says there are three New Testament dimensions to grace: its converting power, its transforming power, and its empowering power.[27] It is not just the power of forgiveness but power to live in a new way.[28] To embrace a biblical understanding of grace is to seek to live in that new way.

Consider what the original readers of the New Testament would have thought when they read, for example, "the wages of sin is death, but the free gift of God is eternal life through

Christ Jesus our Lord" (Romans 6:23, NLT). In their culture, one who received a gift was obligated to respond. The notion of a "free gift" is a modern ideal, not an ancient one. In other words, the gift of grace not only saves us; it also empowers us to live out our response.

REPENTANCE

Contemporary Christians have largely been trained to think of repentance as "turning from" something. We stop sinning, stop watching pornography, stop being angry. A "turning to" is implied and sometimes explicitly described: a life of growing in patience, in kindness, in the fruit of the Spirit. But where we place our emphasis—on turning *from* or turning *to*—makes all the difference.

In Hebrew, the word *repent* (*shub*) means to turn, literally, to another direction and implies going in a new direction.[29] And in Greek, *metanoia* means a change of mind.[30] It refers to a complete change of direction and a complete change of mind, with no limits to the ramifications—an infinite loop of transformation, pointing us to a boundless future.

Repentance is not simply to turn away from; you must turn to something new. Jesus did not just say, "Repent" but "Repent *and* believe the good news" (Mark 1:15, emphasis added). It's an ongoing process of transformation. When I repent, I am not just saying, "God, I'm turning away from my limiting thoughts about you," but venturing into *new* thoughts about God. I repent, for example, of my belief that I am alone in my suffering, even if I feel that I am. Instead, I trust that God is with me, because he says he is, whether I feel it or not. And, more importantly, I share my loneliness or sorrow with others, in the context of Christian community, which is how I demonstrate that my mind is really changing (or that I'm committed to seeing it changed). I refuse to curse life or the world, and I choose hope and trust.

This is far different from believing "I repented and believed in Jesus, so I'm going to heaven when I die." Such reductionism falls woefully short of the biblical picture of repentance. Further, the call to repent means far more than "try much harder to be a good boy or girl."

By reclaiming the words *salvation*, *faith*, *grace*, and *repentance*, we can move closer to the discipleship gospel. Biblical language properly understood creates new and vibrant realities for us. Or rather, it helps us return to ancient realities. Theological revolution in our day comes first by returning to biblical language as envisioned in Scripture itself. But to rebuild the discipleship gospel, we must attend not only to biblical language but also to biblical imagery and metaphor.

REBUILDING THE DISCIPLESHIP GOSPEL: FROM TRANSACTION TO RELATIONSHIP

The Bible is nearly miraculous in how it speaks through not only its language but also its imagery and metaphor. There is no space in this volume to extol its virtue here at any length, so a few brief examples, by way of illustration, must suffice.

Did you know that the only cube shape in the Bible occurs in the Torah, Ezekiel, and then, finally, in the book of Revelation?[31] The first cube-shaped structure in Scripture is the Holy of Holies, the place where God's presence dwells within the Tabernacle. This image reoccurs in Solomon's Temple, the shape of the Holy of Holies (1 Kings 6:19-23). Then, in Ezekiel, the prophet has a vision of a cube-shaped city, which occurs again in the book of Revelation, as a cube-shaped city comes to earth (Ezekiel 41:4; Revelation 21:16). The biblical witness uses imagery—the shape of a cube—to build clear theology. In Revelation, the city (in the shape of a perfect cube) represents the very presence of God, the Holy of Holies, coming to earth. The theology of Scripture is not souls fleeing a burning earth to get to a disembodied heaven but rather a vision of heaven on earth, as God's very presence becomes available to all and in all. The point of the imagery is not a literal measurement of the City of God in terms of cubits or miles; to get mired in that literalism misses the point. Rather, the imagery invites us to imagine the city as the new Temple, filled with God's very presence, which remakes the face of the earth. The Bible says something poetically with imagery, rather than with doctrinal bullet points. In Scripture, a picture really is worth a thousand words.

Jesus, appropriately enough, provides another example. He taught in parable, knowing that familiar imagery and everyday language captures the imagination and is more easily remembered. Brain science confirms what our brilliant teacher well knew: We remember what we can envision. Theology as story is remembered above theology as bullet points. I recently told a story about flying into a rage because hand sanitizer spilled all over my book bag. I stood before a congregation holding up a bottle of hand sanitizer saying, "Can you believe this hand sanitizer did this to me? I'm going to pass this bottle around, and I want you to curse it. Even throw it on the ground and stomp on it, if you like." The point, of course, was that it wasn't about the hand sanitizer at all, but instead a problem in my own heart—anger, and sorrow beneath it, which I had not yet been willing to touch or process. When I returned to that church a year later, I was shocked when someone came up to me and said, "That illustration changed my life. It's not about the hand sanitizer; it's about my own heart." I thought to myself, *But how many other fine points I made in that sermon!* But it was the image that had stuck with him and changed his heart and mind. Jesus knew this above all. We often get bogged down in imageless theology, but imaged theology helps free us.

Language is used to create imagery (like the cube-shaped city) and to tell stories, but language can also get us stuck in old or incorrect metaphors, images, or stories. This is exactly what has happened with much of our biblical language within the Gospel Americana: Our language has gotten stuck in the story, imagery, and metaphor of *transaction* rather than *relationship*.

Transaction sounds like: "You've got the golden ticket now! You've said the prayer; you're going to heaven when you die." Or "If you just do these spiritual practices, your life will be great." Or it might sound like, "If you're a good Christian, you won't really suffer (your kids won't be born with illness, you'll have lots of money, et cetera)." Even the common, yet nonscriptural mantra "God will never give you more than you can handle" is mired in transactional thinking, encouraging us to believe that God somehow causes our suffering and is measuring out the amount we can deal with, rather than being the God who sits with us in sorrow, in the fellowship of suffering.[32] It's not very far from the disciples' question in John 9:2: "Who sinned, this man or his parents, that he was born blind?"

Contemporary theological language has often set up a false

image of salvation specifically as a transaction. *We are sinners. Jesus died for our sins. Receive his forgiveness, and you can go to heaven when you die.* Say the prayer, get the ticket.

The forgiveness of sins must rather be understood within the broader framework of Jesus bringing us into the Kingdom of God. The forgiveness of sins is the *beginning* of transformation, a starting line that we have treated as the finish line.[33] The New Testament describes salvation as a transforming relationship. The imagery used to describe it is relational—adoption, forgiveness, reconciliation, and so forth. Discipleship is thus understood as a relational process: learning to live and love like Jesus while being changed to be like Jesus. In saving us, Jesus has justified us—that is, brought us into right relationship with God.[34]

To use Paul's metaphor, the church is in a marriage relationship with Christ (Ephesians 5:21-33). This is the same metaphor used at the end of the book of Revelation, "the wedding supper of the Lamb" (Revelation 19:6-9). The Scripture gives us a metaphor to understand something that cannot be understood in mere words and that somehow transcends language.

THE HARD WORK OF RECLAMATION

Even when we already believe and ascribe to the reality of the discipleship gospel as taught by Jesus, we are still deeply affected by the culture of the Gospel Americana, even when we have disavowed it. A friend of mine recently taught a Bible study in a room full of Millennials, and she asked, "Why do you follow Jesus?" Everyone in the room said, "So we can go to heaven when we die," or some variant of that idea. No one said anything about transformation or participating with God in seeing all things new. No one mentioned discipleship as a pursuit of the good life.

This anecdote reveals a critical truth: It is not enough to react against something; we must build something new toward which we can move. If that is not accomplished, we will simply drift back into the old perspectives we are most familiar and comfortable with. We think change of belief is all there is. But to escape the allure of the Gospel Americana, we need new language, imagery, and metaphor; only then will discipleship and disciple making as Jesus taught them become normative.

Imagine that you are invited to a party at a beautiful house, with a host and guests you are very excited to spend the evening with. You have heard about this party. Its delights are legendary. So you get all dressed up, dolled up, to the nines. You look "smart," as the British say. Then you get out of your car and walk across the front walk toward the party, open the front door, and cross over the threshold, where you are met with a barrage of lights and colors. People smiling and dancing. And the food. Dear me, the food. It's delicious, more the stuff of a banquet than a party. You move deeper into the house, your host moving with you from room to room, inviting you deeper into the festivities. Each room becomes more alive with the glow of the party, and you lose all sense of time in the joy of it all.

Looking back, the next morning, you would certainly say that the moment you crossed the threshold was a beautiful moment. But it was certainly *not* the point of the party. The point of the party was to celebrate with your host; the point of crossing the threshold was to move deep into the party. Imagine that, after getting to the front door and crossing the threshold, you had decided to stay there, thinking that *that* was the point of it all. Think of how much you would have missed!

By locking up the full-bodied biblical notion of salvation

within a transactional metaphor, this is exactly what the contemporary church has done! We think of salvation as the moment of crossing a threshold, and we let people assume this was the point of it all, that the forgiveness of sins is primarily what the gospel is about, when really, it's about the party and the host—the coming of God's Kingdom under the lordship of King Jesus. We miss that the point of crossing the threshold, as wonderful a moment as it is, is not the point of the party. And to miss the true point turns out to be a great tragedy.

Perhaps the reason the contemporary church is increasingly deemed irrelevant is because it has focused on getting people over the threshold and not into the party—the coming of the Kingdom of Heaven (cf. Luke 14:15). We must change our imagery of what it's all about, so that people understand what biblical language was pointing to all the time: salvation as participation with God in what he is doing in us and in the world.

With proper perspective and prophetic metaphors in place, our thinking and our imaginations are freed up. Indeed, when we change our imagery, our story, and our metaphors, everything changes. Grace, in the context of the party, is not just the power to get us over the threshold, though it *is* and *remains* that. It's also the power of God filling our lives, taking us deeper into the party, empowering us to live as disciples. And two distinct categories—conversion and discipleship—collapse into one movement. Into one relationship.

INTO A NEW FUTURE

Having acknowledged the stuckness of the Gospel Americana, discovered the biblical mind-set that prioritizes both/and thinking over either/or thinking, considered Jesus' ways and means of making disciples, and recovered the fullness of language and imagery the Bible provides, we find ourselves with a more robust, more compelling gospel story to live into and share. We can look to the future with gospel hope for the great commission to be fulfilled—that local movements of disciple making would change the world.

Further, we can rescue the five "gospels" discussed earlier by placing what is true of each in our broader relational story.

The discipleship gospel, we discover, can hold

- forgiveness (but not at the expense of all other aspects of the gospel) *and*
- social action in Jesus' name (to make present the Kingdom of God, not just generic goodness) *and*
- a trust that God cares about our whole being and the whole being of others (and not just the "name it, claim it" imbalance of the prosperity gospel) *and*
- a knowledge that God delights to meet our needs (without buying into the American consumer gospel) *and*
- proper confidence and certainty (not arrogant self-certitude)

. . . all under the banner of the gospel of Jesus, which demands that we follow him and be in his likeness.

Disciple-making movements are not just built on theory, ideas, or language alone but on practices (we will use the terms *spiritual practices* and *spiritual disciplines* synonymously) that lead to transformed disciples and sustain disciple-making cultures and movements. These practices are the focus of the next chapter.

THE PLACE WHERE GOD ALREADY IS

"Listen to the rain, we have so few nights to enjoy rain,"
I said, lying in bed with my wife, back from her dance class,
*   and myself having read, in*
waiting, a book about how Christianity is subversive,
and that we should use cloth diapers on our babies and shop
*   only at co-ops*
And maybe that is true, or some of it,
But I had no energy for the imagination of it
Not even guilt, just too tired to try anything but listening to the rain
When my wife said,
"You know what I pray when I dance?"
All my thoughts hid from her, "No," I said. "What?"
"Lord, give me this dance. Give me this one dance."
I squeezed her leg, because it made sense to me
Somehow, the mystery is:
All we do is enter the place where God already is
the dance, the rain, the tired bed

6

RUNNING WITH HORSES

DISCIPLESHIP PRACTICES
FOR EVERYDAY LIFE

*Nothing less than life in the steps of Christ is adequate
to the human soul or the needs of our world.*

DALLAS WILLARD, *THE GREAT OMISSION*

BRANDON

AS DISCIPLESHIP PRACTITIONERS, we've noticed a growing sense that church as we've known it is dying. In many places, the modes and models of church are simply no longer sustainable.[1] People are not giving money to, let alone attending or participating in, church life as it once was. If the church as we've known it *is* dying, what will be resurrected in its place? Far from seeing the current decline as a death knell and cause for lament, the ringing can be viewed as a birth announcement to welcome and celebrate. There is an exploration for something new—a more vibrant, dynamic, flexible way of doing church in an increasingly post-Christian, post-Christendom world. Leaders are exploring different ecclesiologies, such as home churches or missional communities, or leadership structures, like shared leadership or flat leadership. In the mix of these conversations is a resurgence of discipleship. There is a return to the question "How did Jesus make disciples?" and a recognition that planting churches alone—or even growing large churches—does not in itself lead to cultural change or the revolution that Jesus envisions for the world.

Along with this increased sense that "there must be more" or "we need something new," here are a few other trends we've noticed in the contemporary church:

There is a growing longing for mysticism and mystery. Over twenty years ago, Robert Webber and Lester Ruth noted in their *Evangelicals on the Canterbury Trail* that evangelicals were leaving traditional evangelical churches and joining Episcopal or Anglican churches to add sacramental elements—and with them, a sense of holy mysticism—to their spiritual journey.[2] More recently, the spate of books on the Enneagram reveal people are not just looking for information download via Bible study but deeper understanding of themselves and the world around them.[3] Evangelical churches, as theologian and celebrated author Richard Foster noted, traditionally have focused on "Word-centered life," the proclamation of the gospel.[4] But there is clearly a longing to balance the Word tradition with both sacramental and contemplative elements.

Within the American church, in the last decade especially, there is also a renewed focus on vocation. At the heart of this focus is a longing for the integration of discipleship and spiritual formation into all arenas of life rather than viewing spiritual formation (as, practically speaking, it often has) as a discrete, separate sphere of life. The notion that you live as a Christian "here" (at church and home) but as something else "there" (at work)—or the notion that work is not holy or sacred in and of itself—is dying, thankfully. In its place is a longing for a spirituality that sees all of life as integrated, without stark divisions between the sacred and the secular.

But there is another trend, one that gives us great encouragement. There is a movement toward spiritual practice and the recognition that we must not only be hearers of the Word but also doers, that we must recover time-tested spiritual disciplines that have often been neglected. This is a hopeful moment. Schools of spiritual formation are springing up in churches that had none. One need only look at the surge of Christian books about spiritual practice in the last decade, following in the footsteps of writers like Dallas Willard and Richard Foster, who articulated in cogent language the importance of spiritual disciplines, to see that something new is seeking birth. Anecdotally, in the churches I grew up in, "the prayer of examen," "contemplative prayer," "centering prayer," or "breath prayer" would have raised every red flag, stoking fears of a mystical-and-therefore-dangerous Catholic invasion through which Satan was sneaking into the church (I'm not being hyperbolic, and my church wasn't even the most conservative on the block). More recently, a good friend of mine and fellow pastor was kicked out of his church for bringing spiritual-formation language and practices into his church. Nevertheless, in many churches we visit, there is now a growing culture—or at least a subculture—of spiritual practice, of dissatisfaction with the Gospel Americana. Words like *contemplation* no longer frighten the imagination; indeed, there is a recognition that these are time-tested, ancient practices (contemplative prayer, fasting, hospitality, and so forth) that we must revive. There is a steadily growing movement toward marrying justification by faith with the imitation of Christ.

In this movement toward spiritual practice is recognition of the hollowness of the Gospel Americana and the quest for a discipleship-based spirituality, with allegiance to Jesus in all aspects of life. But what will it take for this movement to become mainstream? For discipleship-based Christianity to become the norm?

This movement toward spiritual practice is a proper reaction against two cultural forces: the disembodiment of spirituality and psychological introspection run amok.

TOWARD AN EMBODIED SPIRITUALITY

The disembodiment of spirituality—the notion that spiritual life takes place primarily in the life of the mind—is always lurking in Western thought, given the dualism (the division between body and mind) popular in Plato and even earlier. But a more recent iteration of disembodiment came in the Enlightenment, through the modernistic belief that rational knowledge and understanding would change the world. Descartes is famous, above all, for his statement, "I think, therefore I am."[5] Descartes was trying to secure a sure footing for epistemology—of being confident in what we know and how we know it. But his statement influenced modern philosophy (and, indeed, was the beginning of modern philosophy) by placing the only knowledge we can be certain of squarely within the individual rational mind. If this is true, what is required is a retreat into the mind, to an inner world of ideas, not unlike we find in Plato, who retreated into a world of forms. According to this perspective, that is the only place truth can be found and known. This is all fine, as far it goes—after all, the mind is, in one sense, the only place we can know anything. But insofar as he de-emphasized the importance of the body or the notion that truth exists "out there," in relationship with others, Descartes represents a movement away from the full embodiment of a Hebrew mind-set, in which truth is less a set of doctrines in the brain but in a real sense a faith we live out, in action and interaction with others. Indeed, as is often said, Judaism has no clear doctrine, creed, or dogma, as such; what it does have is a way of practicing and embodying faithfulness.

The Enlightenment emphasized knowledge not only philosophically but also scientifically. Enlightenment thinkers believed that through scientific inquiry, society would continue to improve, humanity would gradually perfect itself, and a new future would be inaugurated. This optimism came crashing down when the scientific method revealed that the nature of reality is far more complicated than we thought—when

Newtonian physics gave way to Einsteinian relativity, for example. And when peace was shattered by the brutalities of two world wars, the bombs of which signaled a death knell to the optimism of the Enlightenment and the hope of a perfected society. The brutalities of man belied the rosy aspirations of man. But not before the modern focus on right knowledge and understanding was translated into the church.

The modernistic imperative to know became firmly rooted in Protestant evangelicalism: increased understanding of the Bible and how to defend the faith would lead to the good life. Thus, "Bible study" was to become the definitive marker of evangelical faith. In practice, this focus on the life of the mind came at the exclusion of other spiritual practices, further de-emphasizing and disembodying spiritual practice. It's not that fasting or hospitality or silence and solitude ceased to exist, it's just that they became less important in the evangelical hierarchy of value. The Protestant Reformation had already pushed against anything that smacked of Catholic mysticism. Modern philosophy only affirmed and strengthened this movement. If you have the right knowledge and the right apologetics in your head, what need is there to practice it?

The typical form of an evangelical church service, post-World War II, illustrates this belief. In an Episcopal or Catholic service, the homily—a shortened sermon—is not the zenith of a worship service. That right belongs to the Eucharist, or Lord's Table. The average service structure in an evangelical church, on the other hand, was and is: some songs, some church business and announcements, the giving of tithes and offerings, all culminating in a thirty-minute (or perhaps much longer) sermon. What is communicated in such a structure is "learn more about the Bible, and you will be transformed." This makes sense, given the Word-centered focus of evangelical churches. Nor is this emphasis bad or wrong, since being grounded in Scripture is critical for spiritual life (considering that the Scriptures reveal the story of God and his intention to draw the world—and us with it—to himself). But whatever the upside of the Word-centered evangelical tradition, there was a potential dark side: an overfocus on knowledge and a potential temptation to center Christian life on being right and having certainty versus being open to God. The promise of knowing and being certain is a powerful intoxicant, after all—not so different from the original temptation into which Adam and Eve fell: the promise of being like God and, therefore, not having to be dependent on God.

In real terms, the evangelical temptation has been toward a knowledge that can make one certain and therefore right and powerful and away from practices that increase an awareness of vulnerability before God. Dallas Willard, aware of this temptation, remarked, "Bible study is the great enemy of spiritual growth today."[6] If you know Dallas Willard, you know he was not against Bible study. Rather, he was against Bible study as the stand-in for spiritual formation. What is needed, he knew, was not mere knowledge of what Scripture says but actually living out Scripture. This, of course, is a dangerous affair: Jesus did not call his disciples to simply memorize Bible verses but to do wild and crazy things, led by the Spirit of God. These are the very acts that fill the Scripture we study.

The contemporary movement toward spiritual practice is also a movement against psychology run amok. Let us offer a disclaimer that we are not antipsychology. We are protherapy and procounseling, when they are needed. But we are against a variant of psychology that has many tendrils in our world: the psychology of endless inner focus and introspection with the promise that you can figure yourself out. Jesus agrees with Plato: The good life does mean an examined life. But an examined life that just keeps examining itself is no life at all. This is why Dietrich Bonhoeffer was dismissive of psychology as an excuse for people to "busy themselves with themselves."[7] Understanding yourself is important. But it's also important to understand—and accept—that you will never fully understand yourself.

There are limits to our knowledge and to what we can put into language. Spiritual practices are not always about understanding but rather about trusting when we *don't* understand. They are about loving God and neighbor—about praying, fasting, being hospitable, and so on—in ways that don't require us to have everything figured out. In Jewish thought, faithfulness was always about action, about not just being a hearer but also a doer. We are called to live into loving God and our neighbor (Mark 12:30-31), not thinking or even understanding our way into it. As my friend Bryan Rouanzoin says, "Jesus is the way, the truth, and the life, but oftentimes, he is the way before we understand that he is the truth and the life" (John 14:6).[8]

Spiritual practice, then, is about a faithful embodiment of our spiritual life that is not simply about more self-knowledge but instead trains us to love God and others, in practical terms.

HOW ARE WE TRANSFORMED?

A spiritual practice is anything that shapes our body and soul to live the good life, as Jesus taught it. Core spiritual practices are, among others: reading Scripture, praying, observing Sabbath, fasting, living in community, practicing hospitality, and telling the story of God.

But *how* do they transform us? Dallas Willard loved to ask, "How does one naturally become a good person?" This question is at the heart of all spiritual life, since discipleship is always about becoming a new creation. First, we must understand how, scripturally speaking, transformation happens. It certainly does not happen just because you engage in religious activity like prayer or Bible study, as Jesus himself makes clear (Matthew 6:7). So how—biblically speaking—does transformation occur?

One way of understanding transformation is that we are changed by willpower and by working very hard to make good choices. By these efforts, we can shape our souls. And there is some truth to this. Paul tells us to run with all the discipline of an athlete (2 Timothy 2:3-7). There is great effort in the spiritual life, as Scripture makes clear. We absolutely can change our behavior, maybe even the way we think, by trying hard at it. For example, if you are constantly tempted to overeat or to watch pornography or to gossip, you can experience some level of change by applying more willpower into moderation, abstinence, or keeping your mouth shut. You may find peace in the results of this behavior and be motivated to continue. But we all know that willpower, powerful as it may be, is limited. And, in fact, willpower can devolve into a religious game about the effort and appearance of trying to "do the right thing." We get so caught up in our own efforts to be good that we come to think of ourselves as good, and we get offended at any notion to the contrary. Not when we've worked so hard. Jesus constantly warns about this trap in his parables.[9]

Jesus offers a different—counterintuitive—method of

transformation. You are transformed by coming to God and being held by God, but you don't come to God by being strong or by proving how great you are. You come to God by your failure, brokenness, and weakness. You don't come to God by getting everything right; you come, in practical terms, by realizing you are *not* going to get everything right. But this takes a great deal of trust! In fact, it is this trust that transforms us. Or rather, God transforms us as we trust in him. This requires a shift from self-focus to God-focus, which leads us to others-focus, which is the simplest formulation of discipleship. Disciples learn to focus on God and others, losing their small, protective, self-focused lives in the process.

Scripture continually emphasizes our need to be aware of our weakness because it's only in a posture of dependence that we can trust God and thereby leave behind our small, self-focused lives. As Paul said, "I am glad to boast about my weaknesses, so that the power of Christ can work through me" (2 Corinthians 12:9, NLT). He is picking up the theme that Jesus first taught: "Blessed are the poor in spirit, for theirs is the kingdom of heaven" (Matthew 5:3). Blessed are you when you are poor and are aware of it. This is a counterintuitive notion of what "being blessed" is! It's part of Jesus' upside-down Kingdom. In Jesus' world, being rich—and therefore being deceived about what really matters—is true poverty. It's why Jesus taught so often on money and on hypocrisy. When we have money or religious prestige, we often feel very little need to trust God. On the other hand, it takes trust to let God hold us when we are aware of how very weak and in need we are.

Paul also picks up on Jesus' theme of the inability of religious practice to transform us. In the book of Romans, he says that the Jewish law (the Torah) was good and necessary. It taught Israel, for example, that they lived in a moral universe (Romans 7:1-13). It taught them about morality and that there is such a thing as sin. But the law could never *transform* Israel. In Galatians, Paul says it succinctly, declaring the law a "babysitter" (Galatians 3:24, NTE). This is an incredibly provocative statement for an Orthodox Jew to make. The law, after all, was at the center of Jewish life and ritual. But Paul recognizes that the law is only a stage in development. After all, what do babysitters do? They help you mature until you can take care of yourself. In the spiritual life, the law teaches you that you are never going to become good on your own, so you can finally become good in God. Receiving God's love is what makes your heart free and good. Allowing God to accept and adopt you when you are unable to keep the law is incredibly humbling. Again, this takes trust.

Trust is always the key to transformation. We are transformed when we trust who God is and what God says. We are transformed when we hold on to hope amid pain and suffering.

TRUST THAT TRANSFORMS

When my dear friend John was diagnosed with a terminal brain tumor, I spoke with his wife, Barbara, also a close friend of mine, on the phone. I was shaking with sorrow and grief and fear, but Barbara's voice was steady, despite the strain in it. I'll never forget what she said: "We are seeking how to do this— how to talk this out—well." She told me they were trusting God in the midst of deep sorrow. We were all incredibly grateful when we found out that John's diagnosis was not a brain tumor but a serious, though treatable, form of multiple sclerosis.

John and Barb were prepared for their trial. They had long practiced trusting God so that when a moment of trial came, they were ready to trust, despite the horror in their situation.

For me, the last two years of pastoral ministry have been incredibly painful. As we engaged in important conversations about sexuality, our church lost many people. At one point, I began to wonder if I would need to find another job. If it might be the end of our beautiful community as I have known it. This was painful enough, but another pain came in discovering the sharp edge of many of my own internal dysfunctions. One of my survival strategies has been working harder or banking on the belief *I can figure this out* or *If I just perform well enough, I can make this work*. Beneath these beliefs was a darker one: *I can be what people need me to be*. This is not a healthy posture for anyone, let alone a leader. It is a sort of codependency, the belief that I am responsible for other people's beliefs, emotions, or behaviors. At the root of codependent behavior is the belief *If I can make someone else happy, I'll be safe*. Through a season of trial, I was forced to jettison these beliefs. Or, more accurately, to have them pounded and sweated and wrestled out of me. It was painful because, as much as I wanted them to go, they formed a core part of my thinking and, in some way, my identity. I needed them to die—and it felt like a death—so I could enter a bigger story. That story sounds like: *It's not about me. You can't please everyone. And it's not my job to hold everything together*. This brought tremendous joy and freedom, but it only came through the path of suffering and letting go. My suffering pushed me into a place where I had to trust that (1) God was with me, no matter what happened and that (2) it was God's church, not mine. Number two can be a cliché, or it can be a tangible reality. Through the struggle, it became that sort of reality for me. But it was a struggle to trust this, even though I had no other choice.

Trust does transform us. But trust often becomes tangible and transformative only in the face of some struggle or sorrow. As David Brooks says, "If you ask anybody, 'What's the activity that you had that made you who you are?' no one says, 'You know I had a really great vacation in Hawaii.' No one says that. They say, 'I had a period of struggle. I lost a loved one. I was in the Army. And that period of struggle or that period of toughness made me who I am.'"[10] Struggle makes us confront our deep fears—that God is far off, that he is angry, that he doesn't love or see us—and put them to death. In the process, we learn to trust in a different reality in which God is present and near to us in all things. Salvation is built on this deep knowing of who God really is. Many people are converted to Christ in a flash of understanding about who God is, but all of us are being continually converted, always coming into a deeper understanding of God's goodness. It's this increased vision of God, which occurs as we trust, that transforms us from the inside out.

THE FACE OF GOD

This is exactly how Paul describes transformation in 2 Corinthians 3:18: We see God's glory and it changes us.

Trust → Seeing God → Transformation

Sometimes the suffering of life forces us into trust.

Suffering → Trust → Seeing God → Transformation

But we can choose to practice trust rather than wait for suffering. We actively practice trust by engaging in spiritual practices.

Spiritual Practices → Trust → Seeing God →
    Transformation

In a sense, spiritual practice becomes a way of preemptive suffering, providing an opportunity to trust God. This is because spiritual practices disarm us and make us aware of our weakness. For example:

- We fast trusting that we will be abundantly fed not by physical food but by spiritual sustenance from God himself. But in the process, we experience how we rely on food to meet not only our physical but also our emotional needs. Or how, perhaps, we use alcohol to "take the edge off."

- We read Scripture trusting that it is the truth of God. But in the process, we realize how many lies we believe about God and about ourselves. We struggle through our doubts that God fully loves us and that we have been made full coheirs with Christ.

- We practice hospitality trusting that God's presence will manifest in a tangible way in the breaking of bread. And we discover just how inner-directed (rather than others-directed) our thoughts and fears are.

- We pray trusting that God will comfort us and speak to us. And we learn how little power we have to transform ourselves.

Spiritual practices, then, always carry with them a discovery of our weakness and our inability to transform ourselves on our own. They indeed carry their own sort of suffering. They make us confront ourselves. They reveal our inflated view of ourselves. They reveal how small and insufficient we are and how self-absorbed we can be.

These discoveries are painful. But in the weaknesses they expose, we are given a chance to trust God's love, to marvel that God chooses us when we are so insufficient, incomplete, and unworthy on our own. Robert Mulholland says that spiritual practices are a way of cracking our false self.[11] Once the false self is cracked, our true self, created in the image of God, can break through. Paul said we are transformed by contemplating God's goodness with our own faces unveiled. The word for face is *prosopon*, which means both face and presence.[12] We are transformed as we contemplate with unveiled faces, or uncovered presence, when we allow God's glory to reach us not as we think we should be but as we really are. *That's* how transformation happens, when we drop our pretense in the light of his presence.[13] This is difficult for us, a process that demands trust. Only in vulnerable self-exposure can we truly experience that "now there is no condemnation for those who belong to Christ Jesus" (Romans 8:1, NLT). We discover that God loves us, even when we are self-absorbed. It's not our effort but the very nature of love itself that transforms us. There is an incredible joy in this, but yes, it first involves a sort of suffering. It is always both a tremendous joy and a great suffering to receive the love of God. We know that it will change us. Encountering God and God's love means we will suffer; we know this, so we resist it.

No, transformation does not come through mere human willpower alone. It comes as we use our will to trust God. Then God's divine presence and grace transform us as we trust. No wonder the Scripture constantly compares two sources of strength: human versus divine. Paul describes it in Romans 8:8-9 as a life fueled by human effort (the "life of the flesh") or life in the Spirit (AMPC). The prophet Jeremiah gives us these words: "If you have raced with men on foot and they have worn you out, how can you compete with horses? If you stumble in safe country, how will you manage in the thickets by the Jordan?" (Jeremiah 12:5). What is it like to run with horses but to be aware of a power racing beside you that is much greater than your own? Spiritual practices are about becoming open to this divine power. And it is indeed preemptive. Suffering will find us, but by engaging in spiritual practices even on sunny days, we can keep God ever in our minds, welcoming him so that when stormy days come, we are already trained in trust.

The problem is, many people are simply not up for this. It's a narrow, not a wide, path! It's *easier* to focus on willpower and making our lives work on our terms rather than learning to rejoice in our weakness (2 Corinthians 12:9-10). It's easier (in some sense) to focus on successful strategies for church growth rather than on making disciples. Making disciples is messy. Transformation requires real, vulnerable, authentic conversation. It's easier to put someone through a program or a class and call it a day. And if you can provide religious goods and services to people and you know they will pay you and provide you with a job, honestly, why not? But we are not called to just be "Christians"; we are called to be transformed disciples. And we are not called to build churches but to make disciples. To do this, we must teach people to trust. And in practical terms, we must teach them to engage in spiritual practices as a tangible way of expressing their trust.

ANATOMY OF TRANSFORMATION

To understand why spiritual practices are so important, you have to place them within the greater framework of transformation and how it happens. We need to understand where spiritual practice fits in our spiritual journey. In *Conversion and Discipleship*, Bill lays out a simple anatomy for transformation, an understanding of how transformation works.[14] This is based on a classical model of transformation that is as ancient as Heraclitus. And, like all journeys, it begins with a starting point and ends with a destination. After all, if you are going on a trip, you need to know two things: where you are now and where you are going. Then you can figure out how to get there.

Our starting point, simply, is the God-given desire for transformation. Scripture tells us that God's Spirit is working within us, calling us to God (Philippians 2:13). We think we are the ones seeking God until we begin to see that God fully pursues and maintains the relationship. And our destination is, simply, to look like Christ, what Paul calls having Christ "fully formed" within us (Galatians 4:19, NTE). This is having the character of Christ.

Desire → Character

We get there, Scripture makes clear, through grace. Grace saves us but grace also empowers us. This is not a passive process!

We demonstrate our allegiance to Jesus by participating in our transformation, and we do that by engaging in spiritual practices that, when engaged consistently, will become habits.

Desire → Practices → Habits → Character

These habits ultimately become our character. This is the path of transformation.

FUNCTION OVER FORM

But here we must insert a warning. A problem for people engaging in a spiritual practice is becoming lost in the *form* of the practice. People can get focused on "the right way to do this" and make it more about the performance of a practice than on becoming open to God through the practice. When we are focused on the form, spiritual practice can almost become like taking a magic pill. If I eat this pill facing east on the night of the full moon, I'll be transformed! My mom, who grew up Catholic, used to tell me that she was terrified of doing her nightly Hail Marys wrong for fear that, if she messed up a word without knowing it and died in the night, she would go to hell. That's an extreme example; relating to spiritual practice according to form can be far subtler.

Focusing on connecting with God means focusing on *function*, not on the form of the practice. Jesus discusses function over form in the Sermon on the Mount. He says, "Don't pray like the Gentiles, who babble many words and therefore think they are heard because of it" (Matthew 6:5-8, author's paraphrase). In other words, don't pray according to rote form but learn to pray from your heart. The function of prayer is to connect with

God, not to get through a formulaic prayer. Pray simply, he says, like this—and then he gives the Lord's Prayer. The point of the Lord's Prayer is not to memorize it and make it a new form, but rather to engage with it from one's heart. Likewise, Jesus says, "Don't stand on the street corners and pray to be seen" (Matthew 6:5, author's paraphrase). In other words: Don't pray with a wrong motive (to be seen and praised by men). Rather, go into a closet, where you aren't seen, and connect with your Father. This, after all, is the true function of prayer.

Parker Palmer speaks to this reality: "Contemplation can be described better by function than by practice. Contemplation is any way one has that penetrates illusion and helps you to touch reality."[15]

What does he mean? First of all, he is speaking of contemplative prayer here, but we could substitute any spiritual discipline—Bible reading, prayer, hospitality, and so on—in the place of "contemplation." Palmer is directing us away from getting caught in the external form of the practice, and by pointing to "any way" that you become aware of God reality, directing us to focus not on form but on function. How does that play out? Well, you are probably engaging in many spiritual practices in your life right now without calling them spiritual practices. A long walk at the park in which you become centered and more aware of God's nearness is most definitely a spiritual practice. Connecting with your neighbors while your children play T-ball can, likewise, be a spiritual practice.

Oftentimes, our notion of spiritual practice is a form that we don't believe we can actually do, and so we end up avoiding it. For example, because of how Western history has influenced us, we think of spiritual practice as withdrawing to the desert or fasting for forty days, and we think, "Well, who can do that? . . . Not me!" Spiritual practice becomes something "out there" for the mystical set. In other words, we think that spiritual practice is something divorced from ordinary life, another "to do" to do in an already busy life. There is truth, of course, behind the idea that spiritual practice takes discipline. I do wake up early to pray, rather than just waking up whenever I please and calling brushing my teeth a spiritual practice (though I guess taking care of teeth is a spiritual practice, too, come to think of it). But by the same token, we need to explore the ways we are uniquely created to connect with God. If we are to value form over function, we must respect the differences in our temperaments and our personalities. In how you hear God and how I do. And we must put ourselves in the spaces and places and practices where we consistently come into the grace and transforming presence of God.

Furthermore, we need to fight against the idea in Western spirituality that the highest ideal in spiritual practice is "stillness." We think spiritual practice of contemplation means sitting still, largely because of the Greek focus on withdrawing into an eternal word to survey truth. But think about Jesus' life: For sure, he did withdraw into stillness and quiet (e.g., Luke 5:16), but much of his spiritual practice happened in motion, on the road. Even today if you go to the Western Wall you will see Orthodox Jews davening in prayer—moving their bodies in rhythm with their prayer—rather than just sitting still. There is space for both, of course, but we have often discounted movement as less than some implicit ideal. For this reason my friend Mike Goldsworthy focuses on the idea of embodiment within spiritual practice. Every week he makes something with wood, and he uses this as a grounding point for his Christian journey, using bodily concentration as a way of focusing his heart and mind, and the practice of creating to experience the heart of God the Creator. In other words, you can certainly be contemplative while moving. This is important because we are a people who often spend the vast majority of our time sitting still, perhaps staring at a computer screen (as I am right now). Then we are told to sit still and pray and that that's where we will become aware of God. Maybe. But maybe we will become more aware of him when we build something or when we move our bodies.

So, to focus on function over form: If you were taught to read a certain prayer three times while standing on one leg, but you actually become most aware of God when you read it twice jumping up and down, then read it jumping up and down. We are being absurd to make sure the point is clear: discover what works for you and do it. I for one do not really connect with the Ignatian Prayer of Examen, but reading through the Lord's Prayer makes me aware of God's nearness and goodness. So guess which one I pray daily?

Above all, our practice must be doable in everyday life. It must be a practice that is easily integrated into the dust and duties of our everyday coming and going. My friend Catherine McNiel wrote a stunning book on everyday spiritual practice within motherhood.[16] She emphasizes seeing the small things of ordinary life as that which shapes our souls. All of life is mission, for example, not just when we go on a mission trip with our church. All of life is sacred, too, even when we are stuck in traffic on the freeway. All of life can be a domain where we are aware of the holy amid the mundane.

LIFE WITH JESUS
(WHAT KIND OF PRACTICES DO WE ENGAGE?)

Jesus is our example of the good life. Not in the sense that our calling is the same as his—we are not, after all, the Saviors of the world—but in the sense that we are to pursue the core principles which he himself embodied. (And let us remember that some of his closest disciples did share intimately in his calling, even to the point of death.) If Jesus is not only our Savior and our Lord but also our exemplar, let us remember that Jesus, too, had a liturgy—an order of spiritual practices with which he consistently engaged. We know, for example, that he was grounded in Scripture, because he was able to recall it and quote it so effortlessly. We know that he engaged in prayer and that he practiced hospitality and treated meals as sacred spaces.

Henri Nouwen notes a pattern that emerges when you study Jesus' way of engaging spiritual disciplines within the good life. Jesus consistently moved from solitude to community to mission.[17]

Solitude → Community → Mission

The practices in each space are different. For example, in Luke 5:16, Jesus withdrew to a solitary place to pray. But sometimes he took specific disciples into this practice of prayer—for example, Peter, James, and John enjoyed specific, private moments with Jesus, such as at the Transfiguration (Luke 9:28-36). And then Jesus moved into a larger community, with his twelve apostles and the seventy-two disciples (e.g., Luke 9:37–10:24). His life of solitude in God and his life of deep friendship in community helped empower him for a life of mission in which he not only taught but also demonstrated what the Kingdom of God looks like.

The message is simple: We, too, need practices that engage us in each of these spheres.

Mike Breen and the discipleship group 3DM use a triangle to capture this idea: UP at the top of the triangle and IN and OUT on either side of the base.[18] The idea is simple: We, too, need practices that connect us (UP) to the heart of our Father, knit us together (IN) authentic community, and send us (OUT) in love for the sake of the world.

This becomes a helpful grid for organizing spiritual practices, because disciple-making leaders must go downstream into particular practices and, specifically, practices that will shape disciples to lead the good life as Jesus taught it. Some practices (prayer, Scripture reading, et cetera) will probably be universal in any disciple-making plan. But there is always room for differentiation and nuance, depending on context. In a culture of overstimulation and excess like ours, practices like silence and fasting become all the more important.

My friend Bryan Rouanzoin, for example, runs a discipleship/spiritual-formation organization called The Way, and they engage these practices:

- Solitude and Silence
- Prayer
- Scripture
- Sabbath
- Simplicity and Fasting
- Community

Let's map them using UP/IN/OUT as a grid. Of course, a practice may accurately be included in more than one category, or even all three, but we will select just one best-fitting category (as we see it) for each practice.

UP Solitude and Silence, Prayer
IN Scripture, Community
OUT Simplicity and Fasting, Sabbath

You may wonder why we put Simplicity and Fasting and Sabbath under OUT, since such practices might, at first glance, fall under UP. We put them under OUT because in this list, Simplicity and Fasting and Sabbath represent a radical form of witness to a world addicted to more stuff, stimulation, and stress. Sabbath, for example, is a witness to the rest that God gives in the midst of an anxious culture. In this way, it is a unique testament to the reality of Jesus and a God who "gives His beloved sleep" (Psalm 127:2, NKJV) and an invitation to take Jesus' yoke—not the cultural yoke of endless, unsatisfying excess—on them (Matthew 11:29-30).

UP/IN/OUT forms one filter for examining discipleship practices to ground a disciple-making culture, one clearly demonstrated by Jesus himself.

We might also create a filter based on Jesus' teaching on the good life. For example, at Long Beach Christian Fellowship, we describe Jesus' teaching on the good life through three prisms:

THE GOOD LIFE

A life of **ADOPTION** (abiding in our belovedness in God)
A life as an **AMBASSADOR** (making present the
    Kingdom of God)

173

A life of **ABUNDANCE** (listening and responding to
God's Spirit)[19]

Given these goals, we map out twelve practices in three
different categories (The Slow Life, The Grounded Life, The
Generous Life), which can become habits leading toward maturity in each area.

THE SLOW LIFE Unhurriedness, Silence, Sabbath,
Hospitality
THE GROUNDED LIFE Prayer, Scripture, Fasting, Risk
THE GENEROUS LIFE Forgiveness, Gratitude, Giving,
Telling the Story of God[20]

Let's map these practices in two ways, first using the filter UP/
IN/OUT.

UP Unhurriedness, Silence, Sabbath, Prayer, Fasting,
Gratitude
IN Scripture, Forgiveness, Giving
OUT Hospitality, Risk, Telling the Story of God

Now, let us map them according to three dimensions of the
good life we hope to see shaped in the life of each disciple.

ADOPTION Unhurriedness, Silence, Sabbath
AMBASSADORSHIP Hospitality, Risk, Giving, Telling
the Story of God
ABUNDANT LIFE Prayer, Scripture, Fasting,
Forgiveness, Gratitude

The goal for any disciple-making leader is to identify and then teach and embody the practices that will shape disciples to live the good life every day. Our hope is that disciples of Jesus in our context will become grounded in the love of God as they engage in an unhurried life of silence and Sabbath, of prayer and fasting and gratitude, that they will grow in authentic community as they engage Scripture, forgiveness, and giving, and that they will become disciples focused on others—love being at the heart of discipleship—as they practice hospitality, take risks (for the sake of love), and tell the story of God. These are all disciplines that can ground disciples into the good life in unique ways, if they will allow the practices to become habits that shape their lives and become their character.

Clearly, there are different ways to map out spiritual practices based on what works in your context. That's part of the art (rather than science) of disciple making. Disciple-making leaders must be creative in how they describe discipleship and how they flesh out discipleship practices; there is no silver bullet. The main things are to be clear—and to be clear about how these practices lead to the good life as Jesus has mapped it out. And above all, your practices cannot just be about inner formation (grace within us) at the neglect of mission (grace through us). That's why a practice with an inward movement, like prayer, should find coupling with a movement outward, like hospitality.

To reclaim the discipleship gospel, we must ground ourselves not in a theory of discipleship but in the practice of it. This means selecting practices that will shape disciples in the habits of the good life. Still, to create a disciple-making culture, there are two further dimensions of culture building that must be engaged.

CREATING CULTURE: QUESTIONS AND STORIES

We reveal what we celebrate in two ways: by the questions we ask and the stories we tell.

We reveal what we value by the questions we ask. If my wife comes home to show me a new dress and my very first question is "How much did it cost?" that's perhaps not a problem. But if that's my first question every time, I'm revealing that I'm more concerned with money than I am with how she looks or feels in the dress. We reveal operative values by the questions we ask.

In our discipleship process at LBCF, we ask three core questions to reveal what we value. In training disciples to ask these questions, their lives will become continually open to the shaping of God's Spirit. The three questions are:

- God, how can you be so good? (or how are you experiencing the goodness of God?)
- How's it going loving those Jesus has given you to love?
- What is the Holy Spirit speaking to you, and how will you respond?

These sorts of questions—especially the last two—are best asked in community. And asking and responding to these questions is a spiritual practice.

The first question—"God, how can you be so good?"—is a question for reorienting from self-focus to God-focus. We all get so easily self-focused, especially on our faults and failures, and this keeps us from living in the fullness of our adoption in God. But when we ask, "God, how can you be so good . . . to create such a beautiful world, to accept me when I'm still so incomplete and unsorted, to suffer with me when I feel alone?"

we flip our brain to a new orientation. It's like gratitude, which causes the brain to shift on its axis. A new part of our brain lights up when we shift from self-focus to God-focus. Asking "God, how can you be so good . . . ?" is a tool to move out of self-focus or self-hatred and into awe and wonder before God. It's another way to practice trust and openness.

The second question—"How's it going loving those Jesus has given you to love?"—is a core discipleship question. It's the first question we ask at each of our discipleship groups. By asking it first, we reveal that discipleship is not just about our adoption but also about God's grace moving through us as ambassadors of God's Kingdom. Discipleship is about loving others, and by asking disciples to examine how they're loving— what they are holding back, what God is asking them to give, and so on—we invite them into a life of mission. We train them to live into the question at all times, until it becomes a habitual way of thinking and living.

The last question—"What is the Holy Spirit speaking to you, and how will you respond?"—is an all-encompassing discipleship question. We ask this at the end of each discipleship group, and this is where the real tension of discipleship plays out. Following Jesus is not about acquiring more information; it is about responding in obedience to the lordship of Jesus. Discipleship is not about reading a book and calling it a day; rather, the curriculum of discipleship is responding to the work of God's Spirit. By asking this question, we reveal that obedience to Christ—in the midst of a culture that is all about "you do you"—is a core value.

We also reveal what we value by the stories we tell. Stories powerfully reveal values. In fact, they enshrine those values without necessarily making an explicit statement about the value. Imagine, for example, coming to a church's Sunday gathering, where you hear the story of someone who has faithfully served in the church's children's ministry for forty years. Automatically, you know that this community values service and volunteerism (after all, they're taking the time to tell a story about it). Imagine that the next week, a similar story is told. And the same sort of story the following week. Now you're sure, without anyone having said so outright, that this community values service. In fact, telling these sorts of stories is one of the quickest ways to enshrine a value like service in a community; people see what is valued in the community and many aspire to it. Stories set a point of focus on the horizon and ask people to seek that horizon.

But consider, too, what is communicated if stories of service are the only type of story that gets told. What is communicated, for example, if there are no stories about hospitality or loving our neighbors or telling the story of God? That also reveals what we celebrate—or rather, what we are *not* celebrating and aspiring to.

So, sure, tell the story of the faithful children's worker, but make sure you also tell stories that fully reflect the range of discipleship values. Make sure you tell stories not only of someone coming into God's grace (Adoption) but also of learning to live for others (Ambassadorship). Tell stories of someone who took a risk to pray for someone at work or crossed the street to welcome their new neighbors. Or tell the story of someone who learned to sacrifice or be obedient to their conscience, even when it cost them something (Abundant Life).

Don't just celebrate home runs; celebrate big swings. Imagine hearing this story in a public church space: "I crossed the street to talk to my neighbor and . . . it didn't go very well." Imagine the community embracing and celebrating the effort, the big swing, with a "Well done!" What does that communicate? Surely a culture in which it is safe to try and fail and then go again.

Furthermore, communities need to hear stories from the "average Joe," because that conveys that all of us can do this. Discipleship isn't just for super Christians. In fact, your sexiest story is not always the best story to tell. Tell the stories that say, "We can all do this," and tell them often.

If you do these two things—ask questions that reveal values and tell stories that enshrine values—you will create a culture in which all people see themselves as "a royal priesthood" of all believers, from the least to the greatest (1 Peter 2:9). You will be creating a culture in which living as a disciple on mission in God's great world is the greatest adventure.

RUNNING WITH HORSES

Where does all this lead us? Discipleship is not about greatness and success but about faithfulness and fruitfulness. By teaching people to engage in discipleship practices that are integrated into the life they are already living, we can help them learn to trust God *before* and amid life's inevitable sufferings. By cultivating spiritual practices, we teach people not to master spiritual life but rather to learn to be with the Master. This is how we learn to run with horses.

PRAYING IN THE BATHROOM

I like to pray in the bathroom
When I shower or run the water
Or make of it the necessary room it is

It's not a sacred space
Though of course we learn that every space is sanctuary
Everything a burning bush

It's just that
With my hair askance from sleep
My indefatigable cowlick defiant
And my body bulging with new creases
Showing its age as I sit or stand or wash
It seems so much easier to say, with Abram,
"Here am I
And yes, I have nothing figured out
Not today, tomorrow, or yesterday"
And I have learned to say that it's all okay
And that heaven then unfurls all around me
Weightless in my unclenched fists

These words—"Here I am"
Make it so much easier to pray
Make it possible, perhaps,
Since prayer's prerequisite is dropping pretense
And becoming honest
Standing in our nakedness

7

THE
RIGHT
DIRT

The Kingdom of God can't be detected by visible signs.
You won't be able to say, "Here it is!" or "It's over there!"
For the Kingdom of God is already among you.

JESUS OF NAZARETH, LUKE 17:20-21, NLT

BILL

THERE WAS A TIME WHEN SCIENTISTS THOUGHT the secret to life was in molecules, atoms, and other tiny forms of matter. Powerful microscopes made it possible to see smaller and smaller particles, and there was optimism that someday we would find the source. As it turns out, they were right, and they were wrong. They discovered DNA, and it was a marvelous discovery, but it also became apparent that the secret to life was not material but informational. Matter doesn't move on its own; there continues to be the mystery of the Unmoved Mover, the Big Banger behind the big bang. The information contained in DNA was the secret to life. After scientists had decoded the human genome, the director of the Human Genome Project, Dr. Francis Collins (an evangelical Christian), said at a White House ceremony, "We have caught the first glimpses of our instruction book, previously known to God." President Clinton said, "Today we are learning the language in which God created life."[1] DNA is made up of chemical letters, a language, a sequence of letters that makes life possible.

Jesus was the Logos, the Word of God, God's Word to us, the living embodiment of God. He came to us, and we have seen him; we have heard from him. Jesus is the ultimate reality: He is God's answer to our questions, not only in words but in deeds. His Kingdom is a mystery to us. It can't easily be detected, but he claims it is already among us. All reality is word, in language or communication, in the physical realm of DNA, and in the immaterial realm of truth—it is language. That is why Jesus said the Kingdom of God was like a seed that has been sown. "You are permitted to understand the secrets of the Kingdom of

Heaven" (Matthew 13:11, NLT).[2] And that seed was the Word of God. And in the parable of the soils, Jesus teaches us the nature of the Kingdom of God and how it grows. He also tells us what soil we should invest in, what is the right dirt.

> Later that same day Jesus left the house and sat beside the lake. A large crowd soon gathered around him, so he got into a boat. Then he sat there and taught as the people stood on the shore. He told many stories in the form of parables, such as this one:
>
> "Listen! A farmer went out to plant some seeds. As he scattered them across his field, some seeds fell on a footpath, and the birds came and ate them. Other seeds fell on shallow soil with underlying rock. The seeds sprouted quickly because the soil was shallow. But the plants soon wilted under the hot sun, and since they didn't have deep roots, they died. Other seeds fell among thorns that grew up and choked out the tender plants. Still other seeds fell on fertile soil, and they produced a crop that was thirty, sixty, and even a hundred times as much as had been planted! Anyone with ears to hear should listen and understand."
>
> MATTHEW 13:1-9, NLT

What if Jesus had never said any more, answered his disciples' questions, or explained this parable—what would you get from it? My response would be immediate and obvious: "Don't waste my seed by sowing it on rocky or hard ground; make sure to find fertile soil." It is important to think like one of the crowd, who got no further instruction. They went away thinking, *That's good advice, but I already knew that.* The crowd probably had not translated the parable into a spiritual meaning. What seems so clear to the modern reader was not clear to Jesus' audience, including his own disciples. But theologians, pastors, and leaders have spent centuries locked up in silly discussions about this parable and have missed the most obvious point that even the crowd understood—don't waste your time sowing seeds on bad soil; plant in good soil. Understanding the Kingdom of God—and Jesus' teaching—is a process. Those of us reading this passage now need to ask the same question his disciples asked.

> His disciples came and asked him, "Why do you use parables when you talk to the people?"
> He replied, "*You are permitted to understand the secrets of the Kingdom of Heaven, but others are not.* To those who listen to my teaching, more understanding will be given, and they will have an abundance of knowledge. But for those who are not listening, even what little understanding they have will be taken away from them. That is why I use these parables."
> MATTHEW 13:10-13, NLT, EMPHASIS ADDED

Jesus seems to be somewhat of a bad boy—tantalizing peasants with stories they couldn't understand, and because they couldn't understand, if they weren't paying attention, they got no more; in fact, he'd take away any future opportunities to understand. This doesn't exactly match the pleasant, accommodating Jesus that so many follow. He even excuses his elitist attitude with a Hebrew Bible prophecy:

> When you hear what I say,
>   you will not understand.
> When you see what I do,
>   you will not comprehend.
> For the hearts of these people are hardened,
>   and their ears cannot hear,
> and they have closed their eyes—
>   so their eyes cannot see,
> and their ears cannot hear,
>   and their hearts cannot understand,
> and they cannot turn to me
>   and let me heal them.
>
> MATTHEW 13:14-15, NLT, CITING ISAIAH 6:9-10

The words Jesus quotes are from the prophet Isaiah's famous commissioning from the throne-room scene. When the Lord asks, "Whom shall I send?," Isaiah answers, "Here am I. Send me!" (Isaiah 6:8). Isaiah was to preach to the nation of Israel, and his warnings would go largely unheeded. Jesus is saying the same thing about his ministry to Israel. Yes, he had followers, but the nation as a whole rejected him. This is very hard for a person with twenty-first-century sensibilities to accept. Some people just won't understand the words of Jesus or the nature of his Kingdom. And because they don't listen or demonstrate interest, they get left behind. This was not easy for Jesus, for it is well-known that he wept over Jerusalem. He lamented that people didn't understand what they were doing. He desperately wanted to heal them, but they would not let him. Who among us hasn't cried over those whom we love who won't listen to reason or allow themselves to be rescued from self-destruction? It is even more difficult for those who cannot hear and cannot see but don't understand enough to accept that they don't. What can loved ones say? "Listen, my friend, the reason you don't understand the gospel is that you have a hard heart. You aren't really listening to what Jesus has said and is still saying."

LISTENING

What Jesus is saying is easy to miss, but it is the key to understanding. "To those who listen to my teaching, more understanding will be given, and they will have an abundance of knowledge" (Matthew 13:12, NLT).

Listening is more than knowing that your auditory equipment is working and letting the sounds of words pass through your ears. My dog doesn't seem to hear me tell her to stop barking but hears perfectly when I try to sneak candy out of a dish two rooms away—suddenly, there she is, right beside me. The Kingdom of God comes to us in language, in words, or—as Jesus will explain—like a seed that is sown. The key is to listen to the words. As Paul wrote in Romans, "Faith comes from hearing, that is, hearing the Good News about Christ" (Romans 10:17, NLT).

The parable of the sower is about listening. God sows the seed of his Word, and there are many responses. Jesus proceeds, telling his disciples the secret to understanding the Kingdom:

> Blessed are your eyes, because they see; and your ears, because they hear. I tell you the truth, many prophets

and righteous people longed to see what you see, but they didn't see it. And they longed to hear what you hear, but they didn't hear it.

Now listen to the explanation of the parable about the farmer planting seeds. . . .

MATTHEW 13:16-18, NLT

The Kingdom of God can be generally described as "the realm where God's will is done." More specifically, it's the Good News about the rule and reign of Christ in a person's life and, eventually, about his rule and reign over all of his reconciled, restored, and reborn creation. The discipleship gospel is about this process, about how we can join in and become Jesus' disciples. The secret Jesus is revealing is how to access the Kingdom's truth: its nature, how it works, and what we as Jesus' disciples should invest in.

THE KINGDOM'S NATURE

The nature of the Kingdom of God is unlike any normal human kingdom. God's Kingdom is a reality, but often an unseen reality. This is why Jesus said that even the prophets didn't understand its nature. They thought it would be primarily physical: political backed by military power. Most kingdoms come through force, and their leaders are not listeners. But listening is a primary skill in the Kingdom of God—you can't get very far without learning to listen to God. That listening is via language, and the primary language is the Word of God: the living word, the spoken word, and the written word. In human kingdoms, the "best" leaders are the worst listeners. Human kingdoms move forward through coercion, power, celebrity, advertising, and connection. God's Kingdom advances by listening, receiving, and understanding.[3]

Human kingdoms behave like a blunt force, a strong wind, an avalanche, a flood: They sweep into a region, overpower, dominate, create a revolution. Jesus says the Word of God comes like a seed. It is buried in the soil, and if the soil is good, it grows, organically and gradually becoming part of the land, forest, or garden. The human kingdoms of the Soviet Union, Saudi Arabia, and even the United States of America use coercion. Even in the democratic process, 49 percent of citizens are ruled by someone they voted against. But the Kingdom of God operates from the inside out, from changing something within a person to revamping a community to transforming a society to one based on truth. In the early stages, the press cannot report it and writers cannot comment; its secret nature doesn't lend itself to normal metrics. It doesn't seem to us that anything is really happening. It seems so slow, like no progress is being made—in fact, it looks like this Kingdom business is a failure because we are not winning, we are losing. The society is getting coarser and the church weaker, the secularists are increasing and skeptics have free rein in the public square.

Even John the Baptist questioned whether Jesus was who he thought he was. When John was in Herod's jail, he sent a message to Jesus: Are you really bringing in the Kingdom, because I'm about to have my head cut off—are you really the guy (see Luke 7:18-20)? So many Christians who are suffering or who have been dealt a bad hand are asking the same question: *Hey Jesus, if you are at work, why am I in such pain?*

The answer is not necessarily the one we want to hear. When it comes to the long game regarding project Planet Earth, Jesus'

Kingdom doesn't deliver a conflict-free, painless existence to its inhabitants. When a seed is planted, it will eventually change an entire field or forest. A few sticks of dynamite can't change a field the way a seed can transform. Jesus claims that his Kingdom is one of love that creates willing followers—not serfs, slaves, and forced behavior. All human kingdoms will perish, but the Kingdom of God will last forever. Jesus explains the parable, breaking down the types of people who hear God's Word.

IMPENETRABLE SOIL: A HARDENED HEART

> [Jesus said,] "The seed that fell on the footpath represents those who hear the message about the Kingdom and don't understand it. Then the evil one comes and snatches away the seed that was planted in their hearts."
> MATTHEW 13:19, NLT

There are a number of reasons why someone doesn't understand what they hear. For example, I have attended church services conducted in a language I did not understand. I have sat in a room of chemical engineers talking their craft, which I did not comprehend. More pointedly, I have endured meetings where I simply wasn't listening and didn't take in what was said. Is this what Jesus means by "don't understand it"? No, Jesus is speaking of a spiritual condition that makes understanding impossible. In light of the larger context and the quotes from Isaiah, he is referring to eyes that are blinded. Paul recognized this reality as well:

> If the Good News we preach is hidden behind a veil, it
> is hidden only from people who are perishing. Satan,
> who is the god of this world, has blinded the minds

of those who don't believe. They are unable to see the glorious light of the Good News.

2 CORINTHIANS 4:3-4, NLT

It is a hard truth, but truth nonetheless, that many will not understand because it is not in their self-interest to understand. American author Upton Sinclair said it well: "It is difficult to get a man to understand something, when his salary depends upon his not understanding it!"[4] This seems particularly true when religion or politics is debated by professionals who would essentially lose their careers if they stopped and said, "You're right; I'm wrong. My worldview has been changed, and I will conduct my life differently from this day forward." Not understanding has many faces, but the primary reason the first soil does not understand is because it doesn't have the ability to.

Some think of this first soil as not really soil, as if the seed or Word of God falls and does not take root. The text states that it was planted in their hearts. This seems a bit more serious than a seed lying alone on some rocks until a bird (or, in a deeper sense, Satan) comes along and takes it. Some would call this the result of a hard heart, which puts the responsibility on the hearers and what they interpret as the determining factor.

The point of the parable is not for us to take a deep dive into twenty-first-century evangelical theology. The point of the parable is that the seed of God's Word and truth is sown widely, and some of it seems wasted, unheeded by people who are not really listening. It also means that God's Word never returns void (Isaiah 55:11). The Word of God goes into everyone's heart, even of the most skeptical and hardened people. The seed is planted, which is both a comfort and (seemingly) a curse. If everyone can believe, everyone can use reasons for not believing. The fact that the seed is planted in the heart, even of those who cannot understand, makes people accountable. Discussing this further is a deep dive. At least, we must admit that mystery is written all over this. Another factor is that at this sowing of the seed, the people in question were not listening (or they would not or could not listen). But at future sowings of God's Word, conditions might change; those people might listen and find themselves in one of the other three categories.

This first-soil type of person attends your church. They may even serve in some capacity or find their way into a leadership position. Periodically, they will compliment the pastor on his sermon or speak glowingly about a program or an event. At times, they will come under the power of God's Word and will increase their attendance or become more involved in the community. Especially if something difficult comes into their lives, they will be more present. But when the difficulties go away or the novelty loses its appeal, they cool off. They never seem to get into the Bible in a personal way by reading it, memorizing it, studying it, and applying it to life. For these people, the Christian experience remains an intellectual exercise, or even worse, a mystical medicine to rub on when one is in pain. Basically, they don't seem to understand the essence of what it means to be a follower of Jesus. The point Jesus is making about these people is don't invest too much in them. As a leadership strategy, there is very little return on your investment. Give them what they will accept, kindness and a continuation of God's Word. But a leader's special investment of time and effort must be reserved for someone else.

A ROCKY SOIL: SHALLOWNESS

> [Jesus said,] "The seed on the rocky soil represents those who hear the message and immediately receive it with joy. But since they don't have deep roots, they don't last long. They fall away as soon as they have problems or are persecuted for believing God's word."
>
> MATTHEW 13:20-21, NLT

There are as many of these second-soil types in local congregations as there are any other. They are hard to spot at first because they seem to be on fire, all in. Their joy is genuine; that is why it takes a bit of time to discern their shallowness. Generally, it crops up when something in the church community goes a different direction than they had hoped. They might have words with other members or think they were slighted in some way. Because this kind of person doesn't have the deep spiritual resources needed to make it through conflict and benefit from it with a deeper sense of humility and kindness, they normally run away. The simplest way to identify the shallowness is to notice that they are still set on their own agenda and have not found the joy of being dedicated to Christ's agenda for them. They claim to be followers of Christ in practice, but they are looking for a Christ who will follow them.

Frankly, this type of "Christian" wastes a lot of church leaders' time and is the reason why so many clergy want to quit. I recall several times along the way when leaders in the congregation thought we should visit everyone who had left our church because of unhappiness and conflict and find out how we might get them to return. I always said, "No, absolutely not." They would ask why, and my answer was simple and predictive: "Because after listening to them, we wouldn't learn anything new, and we would all want to quit." So if you don't want to find out what a lousy leader you are and you would like to keep your position as a congregational leader, don't spend a lot of time listening to those with shallow hearts. Let me say it again: Save your best time for another kind of person.

NO FRUIT: CONFLICTED HEARTS

[Jesus said,] "The seed that fell among the thorns represents those who hear God's word, but all too quickly the message is crowded out by the worries of this life and the lure of wealth, so no fruit is produced."
MATTHEW 13:22, NLT

One of the ways that the previously mentioned shallow hearts fell away was "persecution for believing God's word." This has become a serious problem in the world of political correctness. I think it is fair to say that a time is coming and is almost here that will make it impossible for a Christian serious about God's Word to hold public office. Add to this working for a major corporation in a significant leadership position. If a person simply believes that Christ is the only way to salvation and holds orthodox positions on human sexuality and ethics, it will make them unemployable. This is why Christians have largely been cowered by the elites of the culture. Many Christians I know are afraid to speak up; they just keep their mouth shut. Persecution is upon us when we are honest with those with whom we interact. Be prepared to be considered antiscience and to be called a hater, warmonger, homophobe, xenophobe, or worse. This will mean that larger numbers of professing Christians will be running for the weeds. But be encouraged: It doesn't need to stay this way. It is not inevitable that everything will get worse—the cultural climate can turn, but it won't be turned by shallow or fearful hearts.

Conflicted hearts are not a lot different. They will be swept easily aside by thorns, worries, and the pursuit of wealth, and because of this, they will not bear fruit. And this is the point, isn't it? Jesus teaches that the first three soils do not bear fruit. I must confess a great weariness in listening to Christian leaders hide their ineffectiveness behind the half-truth that faithfulness is all God asks for. Faithfulness is not enough; fruitfulness is the expectation inherent in the gospel—otherwise, it is not Good News.

What is so good about the religious idea that God loves you and died for you, and that when you die, you go to heaven? If your religion doesn't do something for you now, it has no credibility. If it doesn't improve your life and your relationships now, why believe that, in some magic way, it will in the future? Part of the Good News is that I can participate: I can repent, I can confess my sins, I can join Jesus in his mission, I can follow him, and I can even become somewhat like him and begin to acquire his worldview. And that in some way, when I walk into a room, Christ has arrived. I can reach out and touch my mother, father, sister, brother, wife, husband, son, daughter, friends, and associates.

THE RIGHT DIRT

Jesus has explained the mystery of why so many who hear God's Word fall by the wayside or perform at such a low level. Now he comes to the right dirt, the good soil. From a leadership perspective, this is where you spend your time.

[Jesus said,] "The seed that fell on good soil represents those who truly hear and understand God's word and

produce a harvest of thirty, sixty, or even a hundred
times as much as had been planted!"

MATTHEW 13:23, NLT

"Those who *truly hear and understand.*" The words *hear* and
understand are strengthened by a Greek particle that implies that a
deeper understanding of God's Word leads to a different response.

There are no excuses, problems, persecutions, worries, or
ambitions that would cause this class of people not to hear and
do the will of God. This group is not elite, for they may not be
the most moneyed or educated in your community. The original disciples were not societal elites, but they were available and
all in. What this group has going for them is they understand
what God has said and they are ready to do it.

By this standard of understanding, it is obvious that people
represented by the first three soils did not comprehend the
full meaning of the gospel. The reasons for this are as complex
as human personality, the nature of free will, and the laws of
comprehension. One thing has survived generations, centuries,
cultures, languages, and the rise and fall of kingdoms. That
singular thing is that the gospel requires both believing and
doing. Without doing, you don't have believing, and without
believing, there is no doing. People represented by this final soil
are doers. They will be truly faithful in that they will be fruitful.

A BULLETIN TO LEADERS EVERYWHERE:
INVEST IN THE FOURTH SOIL!

The reason churches do not experience reproduction and multiplication is that we spend far too much time with the first
three soils. What is clear about the first three soils is that the

people they represent are neither faithful or fruitful. Think of this practically. Let's say you have one hundred people in a congregation. There is no reason from the text to believe that each soil represents four groups of twenty-five each. The only way to gauge how many are in each group is by observation and interaction. One recent study revealed that 87 percent of people cite their own lack of commitment, 85 percent say they are too busy, and 70 percent refer to sinful habits as the reason for not engaging in discipleship.[5] Based on fifty years of experience, I believe that the first three groups compose at least 50 percent of any given congregation.

WHAT DRAGS PASTORS DOWN

One of the difficulties of pastoral work is preoccupation with the first three soils. The unhappiness, the pathology of these groups can drain all the human resources from leadership and destroy the focus of the faith community. Many a church finds itself in a crisis based on the immaturity of members who find their own agenda more important than what is for the common good. The very tough reality of this is that most of these people move on to another church and, ten years later, can't even recall what they were so mad about. When you live long enough, you begin to attend their funerals and these disagreements mean even less. I don't hear funeral sermons where the family has instructed the pastor to set things right about that conflict over whether there should have been a trustee board included in the constitutional reorganization twenty years ago.

Dallas Willard once quipped that "th[e] established order can actually keep pastors or teachers in a church setting from thinking of making disciples."[6] The recommendation is not to ignore legitimate needs of the first three soils; it is to invest in the fourth soil. Investment in the fourth soil is what gets squeezed out. The life that is choked out is the growth and development of those who will prove to be fruitful, those who will reproduce, and those who know how to train others so you get multiplication. You can't become a multiplying ministry unless you invest in the fourth-soil people. And the reason that multiplication is such a rarity in the West is because we rarely do it. The gold standard of American Christianity must change from growth by addition to growth by reproduction and multiplication. If we don't do this, we will continue to fail. Jesus commanded us to make disciples of all nations. That was a strategy to reach the world, not a command to be better people or more mature disciples, to get closer to Jesus and feel warm all over. It was a command to move out in obedience and find new disciples who you teach and train to be reproducing disciples and who create movements of multiplication. If we waste our time and resources on the first three soils, we are disobeying, and we will fail—are you tired of failing?

TIMID TIMOTHY

Not everyone is cut out to lead. That is truer than most of us think. Leadership is for everyone only in that every person must lead themselves or their spouse or children. But as the number of people needing to be led increases, those with the ability to lead them decreases. Timothy was not a natural leader. He had some leadership gifts, but he also struggled with some liabilities. Timothy was selected to follow Paul as the pastor of the church in Ephesus. To be fair, he obviously had some wonderful traits, or he would have not been chosen. Paul spoke very highly of him and sent him into some very difficult situations, especially Corinth (1 Corinthians 4:14-18).

We do know that Timothy was young and that following Paul was inherently difficult. Timothy was timid, and he was sickly (1 Timothy 5:23-24; 2 Timothy 1:7). It doesn't appear that Timothy found leading with a strong and principled hand very easy. Otherwise, the exhortation "For God has not given us a spirit of fear and timidity, but of power, love, and self-discipline" (NLT) would not have been issued. This is not something Paul needed to hear because it all came quite naturally to him. All one needs to know about Paul's basic personality is "But Saul was going everywhere to destroy the church. He went from house to house, dragging out both men and women to throw them into prison" and "Meanwhile, Saul was uttering threats with every breath and was eager to kill the Lord's followers" (Acts 8:3; 9:1, NLT).

There is plenty of Timothy in many of us. And this is particularly true when it comes to setting an unnatural course and sticking to it when others resist. This is exactly what Paul was telling Timothy to do, and he needed to be reminded. Timothy didn't need an exhortation to buck up and get some backbone; this would have been wrong for his temperament. Paul's exhortation appealed to their deep relationship: "Timothy, my dear son, be strong through the grace that God gives you in Christ Jesus" (2 Timothy 2:1, NLT).

This unnatural course would be to invest in the fourth-soil type of person who could do what needed to be done. Yes, there were the daily duties of pastoral work, but with Timothy, like with many, investing in those who would be most fruitful was being neglected. Paul was expert in this, as is evident by his own ministry in Ephesus. For two years, he held daily five-hour teaching sessions in the lecture hall of Tyrannus,[7] and he sent out teams of trained leaders who evangelized the surrounding regions and planted many churches (Acts 19:1-41). Paul organized and ran the fifteen-plus churches he had personally started during his missionary journeys.[8]

Quite often, authors of books such as this are written by naturals: What they advocate is their natural inclination. What Paul was telling Timothy he must do began with the resource he already had. Timothy would need God's grace. He possessed God's grace in the past; now he needed God's grace in the present. (Timothy, you need God's help and mercy to get this done. It will not be easy for you.) What was this task that could be quite difficult for Timothy? For you? For me?

> You have heard me teach things that have been
> confirmed by many reliable witnesses. Now teach these
> truths to other trustworthy people who will be able to
> pass them on to others.
>
> 2 TIMOTHY 2:2, NLT

An interesting aspect of Paul's statement is that he started with an apologetic regarding the credibility of his teaching content. Paul wrote almost as though he were in a court of law. Timothy had heard Paul's teaching, so why did Paul reference "reliable witnesses" who had confirmed his veracity? I doubt that Timothy doubted the value of Paul's teaching. It seems Paul was speaking to skeptics and critics in the Ephesian church who doubted Timothy. Paul was not only writing to Timothy— there were other readers of this document. Those other readers would have been Timothy's elders, his advocates, who had contact with the remainder of the congregation. These words were not for Timothy alone. Paul knew Timothy could use all the help he could get to pull off his mission. The stakes were high. One thing Paul could not allow was for the Ephesian church to become a nonreproductive shell of what it once was. We already know that near the end of the first century, this congregation had lost its first love (Revelation 2:4).

Paul was also saying, "My teaching works—my teaching is consistent, it is true to life and to the experience of those who follow it." This is similar to Paul's defense of his teaching to the very volatile Corinthian church. "That's why I have sent Timothy, my beloved and faithful child in the Lord. He will remind you of how I follow Christ Jesus, just as I teach in all the churches wherever I go" (1 Corinthians 4:17, NLT).

Paul's exhortation was heeded because Timothy became a reliable witness himself. What exactly was Timothy to do that would require more resources than he naturally possessed? Paul went on to tell Timothy that investing in fourth-soil, fruitful, trustworthy people would require the **dedication** of a soldier, the **discipline** of an athlete, and the **patience** of a farmer (2 Timothy 2:3-7). The answer? Create a workable plan to invest in fourth-soil leaders who could teach others, as well. Build a discipleship infrastructure that would create multiplying leaders and thus a movement in that region of the world. Paul had already done it once, but now it was Timothy's turn. Why, again, didn't Paul's ministry infrastructure last? It didn't—they never do. Here's the rule: If it's not being done now, it isn't being done at all. It doesn't matter now if it was done in the past; it only matters if someone is busy leading and building it now. It is a myth that a good system will continue when those who make it work leave. When they leave, it slowly ebbs and finally disappears.

When we speak of salvation by discipleship alone, this is the discipleship we are talking about. This is the working out of the entire congregation's salvation with fear and trembling (Philippians 2:12). People will naturally resist this, but it is exactly what Jesus taught his disciples, and what his disciples taught their disciples, and what Jesus personally taught Paul, and what Paul now taught Timothy (Galatians 1:12).[9]

DON'T WASTE YOUR TIME ON THE UNFAITHFUL

The reason it will be resisted is because it requires sorting out the faithful from the unfaithful. The church at Ephesus was not a superchurch. It was small enough that the serious candidates for such work would know each other. You might recall the Ephesian elders and their important role in Paul's life (Acts 20:31). They probably saw themselves as mentors to Timothy, certainly not people who could be taught by this young man. Timothy was being asked by his true mentor to select the faithful people in the congregation who had proven themselves the most reliable and eager. If the Ephesian church was like any church I have known or even heard of, many of the historic leaders were not as open to learning as they once had been. This is why Paul urged Timothy not to let others look down on his youth, why he told him not to scold older men and to treat older women with great respect. Timothy was facing a different dynamic than Paul ever did. Paul was their spiritual father and an apostle; Timothy was just one of Paul's boys. If you draw together the advice Paul gave Timothy, you get the idea that this timid young man with a nervous disposition and stomach was shaking in his sandals.

Timothy needed to select a few people who were the most teachable, eager, and faithful to start teaching them this proven, special curriculum that Paul wanted taught in every church. And doing so would cost him something, because he would be criticized. There would be tension. Timothy was not to waste his time with the semiobedient, the proud, the passive-aggressive resisters. (Make your choice, young man, and move forward.)

THOSE WHO ARE ABLE TO, TEACH OTHERS ALSO

Not everyone is able to make this leap, and even more are not willing to pass it on. Unable and unwilling: They need to be sorted out. Timothy was required to choose those who were faithful, and then—an even more difficult task—those who were able to teach others, and then, one more step, those who were willing to reproduce.

A FAITHFUL/TRUSTWORTHY PERSON

In this context, *faithful* means two things. First, these believers are faithful to the life they have been called to by Christ. Their heart's inclination and their life choices have proven to all those around them that they are faithful to Christ and his teachings. The second aspect regards how these believers have handled responsibility. Can they be counted on to do what they have agreed to do? Are they faithful to commitments? Do they show up on time and complete the work they promised? It doesn't matter if a person is gifted beyond measure or popular for entertaining others, if they can't meet the faithful test, you dare not choose them—they are nonstarters. It is one of life's conundrums that this rule is regularly and blatantly violated by leaders around the church world. The best explanation for such stupidity is that in the spiritual, immaterial world, there are few seen consequences. At work, consequences are immediately seen because they cost money and can be easily measured. In the Kingdom of God, however, sowing and reaping is a much longer process.

ABLE TO TEACH OTHERS

Ability, in this case, means that they have enough leadership ability and passion to communicate the curriculum to others. I have known some gifted teachers, and even ordinary teachers, whose hearts are not on fire, and their words fall short of other people's hearts. If a person who can teach is only teaching in the context of a formal structure but does not communicate to others in their ordinary life, that person is unqualified to teach others. The reason for this is obvious: People imitate and want to be like people they admire. This is what got me moving ahead as a young Christian. There were people whom I admired. I wanted to read the books they read, go to the meetings they attended, and proclaim Christ like they did, because it was all so real, so filled with life, so transformational—that is what I wanted, more than anything. One thing I am sure of: This ability to teach others is not about a spiritual gift of teaching. It helps if you have it, but without the passion, it doesn't even matter—in fact, it makes you dangerous.

WILLING TO PASS IT ON TO OTHERS

It is easy to mumble the last few words of Paul's sentence, "pass them on to others." It seems like a given, but it is not! Ask any leader, and they'll tell you that the hardest thing about leadership is self-accountability to be a good example to the church (1 Peter 5:1-5). I say this with a trembling heart: So many of us fail here. We teach others that they should reach their friends, neighbors, and associates but fail to demonstrate what we advocate. Before we throw in the towel, let me say that the key here is to sense the responsibility and daily offer up ourselves to God to reach out and love as Christ loved.

Here is what I have encountered with my fellow followers of Jesus: We tend to talk about it and even to have the skills to do so, but in the end, to not do it. What we are talking about here are two separate things, even though they are related. The first thing is what Paul is asking Timothy specifically to do. He is to develop an organized group of faithful people who are willing to be trained in a specific curriculum that would be replicated in other faithful people and then again to still more faithful people. They would be willing to teach others to do the same, and the job would not be complete until the person they taught has taught another person. That is called reproduction. When enough faithful people have been taught, then the math takes over, and it transforms into multiplication. The second thing that is connected, of course, is the ordinary lives of those same people being faithful witnesses of Christ our Lord. That is the end game: transformed lives from which Christ spills out in the world.

Why have most not done what Paul told Timothy to do—and, de facto, told us to do? It gets back to the gospel we believe in. A transactional gospel that is only focused on forgiveness of sins can't and won't motivate the church to fulfill the great commission and love the world as Christ loved the world. That is why the church has been satisfied with spiritual addition, because simply having more people in church this year than last has been certified as the gold standard for success. Such non-discipleship gospels fall short because they don't form a basis for obedience to or fulfillment of the great commission. The great commission calls for men and women who are already disciples to make disciples of every nation, every people group on earth. That will require what over 80 percent of churches don't have—more disciples, many disciples, and most of all, new disciples. The great commission is a strategy for reaching the world that requires multiplication. That is why our salvation is linked to discipleship alone—*we can never say we are doing everything that Christ commanded until we have a gospel that incudes discipleship as a natural part of salvation.* And that process begins right where Paul tells Timothy it must: Take what I taught you and teach it to men and women willing to teach others and to replicate it, to multiply it throughout the whole earth.

SOCKS

My clean socks smell of fields brought into order
Dirt, tamed by cotton
And cotton claimed by the long hands of workers who sewed
    the stitches
As faithful as a conductor's watch
As faithful as the baton of Brahms

Oh, I know they were made by machines
But the touches of those long needles moving tirelessly, like the axis
    of earth,
Always follow the hands of man, which first break the ice that we
    pass through
All things made and crafted, for our quickly-passing-through

So that young feet growing old, like mine,
Can find purchase, warm and dry, in one eternal moment
In all the wonder, treading the scent of mud and rock and
    so much green,
And the longing just above the next rise
And the next one, not so very far behind

Conclusion

DECIDE

A human can very well do what he wants,
but cannot will what he wants.
ARTHUR SCHOPENHAUER,
PARAPHRASED BY ALBERT EINSTEIN

ARTHUR SCHOPENHAUER was a German philosopher who lived from 1788 to 1860. He influenced Friedrich Nietzsche, Sigmund Freud, and Albert Einstein, to name a few. One of the things he was famous for was his attempt to discern a person's will and choices.

For example, there you sit, listening to a speaker telling you that thousands of men, women, boys, and girls die every day and go to hell. The speaker peppers the message with heart-rending images of misguided, uninformed people who have no hope unless we get out of our chairs and proclaim the gospel to every person on earth.

Schopenhauer says that my will protects me from the guilt of not responding to the message. What the philosopher is saying is that it only appears that we have free will, that what we end up doing is predetermined. This is the conclusion of a great secular mind. The apostle Paul presented us with another option.

As the Scriptures say,

> "I will destroy the wisdom of the wise
> and discard the intelligence of the
> intelligent."

So where does this leave the philosophers, the scholars, and the world's brilliant debaters? God has made the wisdom of this world look foolish. *Since God in his wisdom saw to it that the world would never know him through human wisdom,* he has used our foolish preaching to save those who believe.

1 CORINTHIANS 1:19-21, NLT, EMPHASIS ADDED

Philosophers have constructed many theories about why and how the human decides and acts. These philosophers are extremely smart and have been largely sincere. Their starting point, however, is rejecting divine revelation as a serious source of knowledge; they have depended entirely on reason. Reason is a gift to humans, but it is limited, flawed, and damaged. Another factor that distorts reason is human biases, resentments, and conflicts. People most often find what they want to find. Finally, what makes the reason project a failure is that God has determined that worldlings will never know him based on reason, logic, and human wisdom. So the answer to our query—Do our choices change history or other people's decisions and eternal destiny?—cannot be answered by reason alone.

There are three ways of knowing: faith, reason, and experience. For a skeptic or secularist to know anything, by their own standards, their arguments must be waterproof. As Lesslie Newbigin believed, "The Greek civilization for all its glory finally perished through a failure of nerve, because at the end of the day the struggle to know the truth was given up as hopeless and Greek civilization relaxed into polytheism and syncretism."[1] This capitulation continues to be practiced by Roman Catholic seminaries, which require students to take a three-year philosophy course before they can begin theological studies. The reason for this to "lay a foundation" for theological claims. This is a product of the Enlightenment and is a capitulation; it is the church agreeing to play the truth game by the rules of the skeptics. This means that "the proofs for the existence of God must be invulnerable—but of course, they are not."[2] Lesslie Newbigin tells a story that makes the point.

There was a great debate held on that subject [Can we escape from skepticism?] in Paris in 1628, when a famous speaker addressed the meeting and claimed that there is an escape from skepticism because we can have probability, and probability is sufficient. And the address was a great success, and there was a standing ovation except from one young man, who did not join in the applause. And the Cardinal Archbishop of Paris, who was there, went over to ask the young man, "Why do you not applaud?" And the young man, whose name was René Descartes, said, "Because if you follow my method, you can have certainty."[3]

Certainty is a philosophical aphrodisiac, and the archbishop was taken with Descartes's idea.

The result was that "the Archbishop gave Descartes a commission to prove certainly the existence of God."[4] He famously began with the one thing he could prove, "I think, therefore I am." When Descartes was done, he had not proven God on a rational basis, and he had effectively separated faith from reason. The Christian way has always been faith and reason working together. No human will ever achieve proof for God by reason alone because God has made sure it can never happen. We get to know God on his terms, we don't make the rules, we don't have the knowledge, and our wisdom is foolish compared to his.

If you, the reader, decide to change your life or alter your behavior, you require some combination of faith, reason, and confidence that God has a plan for you. There is something else: If I answer the call, will it really make a difference to all those hell-bound people the speaker has described?

A couple of Sundays ago, I turned to my wife after the benediction at our church. The benediction says, "The blessing of God Almighty, the Father, the Son, and the Holy Spirit, be upon you and remain with you forever. *Amen*."⁵ Add to that a passage we read that day, an amazing description in Revelation 7:9-17 of the throng of saints surrounding the throne in God's temple, worshiping him day and night. Add to this a crowd of saints too large to count under the altar, who had been killed during the Great Tribulation. They wear white robes cleansed by the blood of Christ, and he wipes every tear from their eyes.

The idea of worshiping God forever was on my mind. "Jane, don't you think God would get bored with people worshiping him forever? Wouldn't he say, 'Enough already, I'm not that insecure—after all, I'm all about humility'?"

Jane chuckled. "You are really thinking like a human, aren't you?"

I had to admit that I was. I was allowing reason and logic and my own human experience to dictate my thoughts. What we are wrestling with is the question: Do my decisions matter, and do they make a difference? I needed to be reminded that reason is part of my decision making, and so is life experience, but at the base of it all is revelation—that is what separates true believers from everyone else.

As you come to the end of this book, what are you going to do, and how will you make that decision? Will you think of discipleship as the key to fully experiencing your salvation? Will that in turn cause you to change your priorities, rearrange your schedule, or alter your finances? I want to start with a statement Paul made that most of us know about. Many of us cherish it; for others, it has become a cultural cliché. Without it, you won't have the confidence to make any decision. You will sit frozen, unable to decide because the ramifications are terrifying.

> And we know that God causes everything to work together for the good of those who love God and are called according to his purpose for them.
>
> ROMANS 8:28, NLT

One of the unintended consequences of the Reformation was a changed focus from the common good to the individual. The priesthood of all believers joined to individual salvation shifted the focus of Christian thought and exegesis. The value of individual opinion became paramount, and the priestly class no longer interpreted Scripture for people. We are—especially now, in the twenty-first century—encouraged to find our own truth, to think for ourselves. So I start freelancing in church based on my reasoning abilities, and my wife must remind me, "You are but a man!" Twenty-first-century humans argue that divine sovereignty and man's free will are contradictory and must be sorted out. Contemporary skeptics, like skeptics of old, love to put God in the dock and interrogate him. And if they can't make sense of God, they reject him because skeptics now have the same problem as skeptics of old: arrogance and a commitment to reject divine revelation.

DOES GOD CONTROL EVERYTHING?

I get a bit creeped out when I hear the cliché "God is in control." Frankly, it is of very little comfort to hear such a thing when the wheels just came off your life. The statement under consideration is "We know that God causes all things to work together for good . . ." (Romans 8:28, NASB). The fact that God is in control does not mean that we have protection or are excused from suffering. It means that there is a limit to what evil can do and that ultimately, its effects will be reversed and justice will be done.

God takes everything that happens, good and bad, and makes something useful and good for all people who love him and are called by him. Without this knowledge, even the simplest decision could create clinical anxiety.

Paul is talking about knowledge that he conveys as commonplace. We all know his claim that God works everything for our good to be true from life experience. It is a knowledge that combines faith and reason. For example, someone might say, "I prayed that something good might come out of a tragic death or illness, and I can identify several ways that it did." That is a knowledge that any believing person can possess, and they are a witness to how God caused a bad situation to turn into goodness.

What is it that Romans 8:28-30 is teaching? Here's some perspective from Tim Keller:

In the Bible, it's never either/or—never. From the beginning to the end, in principle and in practice, it's always this: You are free, and you are responsible, and your choices matter, and you're responsible for your choices, and no one is forcing you to make those choices. And yet, every single thing that happens as a result of those choices is working out exactly according to the plan of God.[6]

As Mike Wilkins once stated, "I live as though both were true."[7] J. I. Packer, in his little jewel, *Evangelism and the Sovereignty of God*, calls this an antinomy, an *apparent* contradiction.[8] We don't have the perspective to figure out exactly what our decisions mean and how they alter reality. At the same time, we are required to believe that God is at work. "If you believe that everything is fixed, despite our choices, you'll be passive. If you believe that our choices actually determine the future, then you should be paralyzed."[9]

Keller paraphrases a short story from Ray Bradbury that considers the unanticipated outcomes of time travel. The traveler is advised to "not get off the path."

> Say we accidentally kill a mouse, one mouse, by stepping on it. That means all the future families of the families of the families of that one mouse. With the stamp of your foot, you've annihilated a billion possible mice. They're all gone. And what about the foxes that will need those mice to survive? For want of ten mice, a fox dies, for want of ten foxes, a lion starves. And eventually, some caveman goes out to hunt for food, but there is no food because you stepped on it. So the caveman starves before having any children, and from his loins would've sprung ten sons, and from their loins, one hundred sons, and thus onward. A billion people unborn are throttled in the womb. Rome never rises on its seven hills. Step on a mouse and you crush the pyramids, Washington never crosses the Delaware, there is never a United States. So stay on the path . . . never step off.[10]

"Every single thing in history is interlocked, interlaced in a million infinite number of ways," and God is working it all together. "You don't have a millionth of the wisdom necessary to make those choices. . . . You should be paralyzed if you really believed that your choices determined the future. Free will, if that was the case, would be the most horrific gift. You shouldn't even get out of bed in the morning."[11]

THE GIRL ON THE FLOAT

It was a crisp Saturday morning in the autumn of 1967, and Gary Jones and I had just finished basketball practice. It was homecoming weekend, and Gary and I rushed to the main street to watch the homecoming parade. Bands and floats passed by, and then I saw her, this most beautiful woman seated on a float, giving that royal wave. I asked Jonesy, "Wow . . . who is that?" Just then, I noticed her name on the side of the float: Jane Johnson. My next thought was: *Anyone that beautiful and classy must be taken.* Not one to be rejected, I asked Gary to check out whether she was dating anyone. Gary reported back that she went on a lot of dates but had no one special. I asked her out, and we started dating. On about the third date, I mentioned that we should go to a dance. She said, "I don't dance." I offered to teach her, and she informed me that it was a religious thing, a Baptist thing. I must admit that my heart sank. She seemed so perfect, but religiosity ruined everything for me. This was the kind of girl who had standards, and I didn't know if I met those standards. I thought church was boring and that most of the young men there were, as I called them, "dorks."

I went to church with her. It was the first time I had done that in ten years. We continued to date for a couple of months, until I broke up with her. I saw her regularly on campus with other guys. She had no problem finding dates. That seemed to be the end of it—except that I still knew there was no other person like her.

At the end of May, it was graduation night. We would graduate, and the next morning I would leave that college for good. Jane would head to Kansas to finish her degree, and I would head to another college.

Jonesy and I were hanging out that night, and we heard that a bunch of girls had rented a hotel room and were hosting a party. We showed up, and the room was filled with forty-fifty young adults. I got right into it and was talking with some girls. I happened to be lying on the bed. Just then, Jane walked through the door, and it was as though my mother had walked in. I sprang off that bed, and it was like she was the only person in the room. Jane and I talked for a very long time, and then I invited her outside. We found ourselves in each other's arms, and before we parted, we promised to write over the summer.

I returned home to Indianapolis and Jane went to her summer home in Grove, Oklahoma. I did write to her, and she wrote to me. Once back in Indy, I decided not to fulfill my commitment to play basketball at the upstart basketball powerhouse Oral Roberts University but to take up an offer from Drake University in Des Moines. I informed ORU that I planned to attend Drake instead, and that seemed to be the end of Bill and Jane as well. I knew that ORU meant great basketball, but it also meant the honor code, which would curtail some of my favorite activities.

Then my junior-college coach, Cletus Green, and the Oral Roberts coach, Bill White, informed me that they were driving to Indianapolis to see me. After dinner, we went to their room at the Holiday Inn. They talked to me about fulfilling my commitment to ORU. Cletus Green told me it was the right thing to do. Coach White told me how important I would be for ORU and how unimportant I would be at Drake. Then the big surprise came up. Coach Green said, "Hey Bill, how about your girlfriend—Joany, Janey, Janice?" It was obvious that he was grasping at straws. "Would she like to go to ORU?" The coaches laid out a plan where she could get into school with a job and some scholarship funds. I played it cool, saying I would call her and ask.

I called her. Her mother answered the phone and said Jane was not home. In those days, long-distance phone calls were a big deal, and I asked when she would return because I really needed to talk to her. Jane's mother admitted that Jane was down at the lakefront with another guy. She went and got her, and Jane came to the phone. I wasn't particularly concerned because I was sure that she would say no and that I would be on my way to Drake University.

She said yes, she would go to ORU with me. I felt bad for the guy standing on the dock waiting for Jane to return. Because Jane said yes, I had to go to ORU myself.

It turned out that Jane didn't have enough scholarship funds to make it work. I called the coach, and he was able to get her a bit more of a loan. I thought that settled it. I went to Tulsa, and Jane was going to travel to campus with her mother a couple of days later. But back home, Jane was unsettled, not sure what she should do. She kept changing her mind: One day, she wanted to go to Kansas, the next day, to ORU. Decision day finally came. Jane's mother told her that she needed to leave a note to her father saying which school she would attend because if she went to Kansas, her mother would need to stay overnight. They left a note that said Kansas and started the twelve-mile drive to the Will Rogers Turnpike. As they neared the turnpike, Jane's mother said, "I think you should go to ORU. I think that is what God wants you to do." So they turned the car around and returned home to replace the note that read "Kansas" with a note that said "Tulsa."

When I saw Jane roll into the ORU parking lot, I knew nothing of the drama. I thought, *Of course she is here; after all, I'm here.* It was all so logical. There Jane and I were, hand in hand, strolling around the ORU campus, and we'd live happily ever after, right? Ten days later, I broke up with her. Jane had let her guard down and started caring for me, and now I had rejected her once again. She was determined to leave ORU and drive north to Kansas. But Jane had a roommate named Vange who told her that no one goes to ORU unless God sends them and she dare not leave. Two months went by, and Jane was dating a very nice-looking farmer from Arkansas. I saw them around campus, and they seemed very happy. I was just freely floating around, doing whatever pleased me. Then one night, my roommate informed me that he had seen Jane and this farm boy kissing in the prayer gardens. I suppose something other than prayer does take place in those holy gardens. After the lights went out and I was lying in my bed, it struck me power-fully what a jerk I had been and how my life was a waste. I was, as Pascal said, licking the earth.[12] I had twice led Jane on and twice rejected her. I needed to get serious about my life. I slid out of bed and dropped to my knees. I asked God to forgive me. I asked God to allow me to live for him, to make my life mean something, and I asked that Jane would forgive me too.

The very next day, I found Jane and told her that I had become a Christian. She was unimpressed, for two reasons: First, she didn't really understand that Christ could change a person. Second, I was a chronic liar. Most of my reasons for breaking up with her had proven to be lies, so why would this tale be true? I begged her to just go on a date with me and let me explain myself.

Jane did grant me that evening, and she decided to give me another chance. A few months later, we were officially engaged to be married, primarily because Christ began to work powerfully in both of our lives. In the summer of 1968, I went to Africa with a mission team from the university. In Nairobi, Kenya, I quite accidently was asked to give a sermon to a village full of residents. The entire village decided to follow Jesus—that is what they said, at least. That July day in East Africa, it struck me that God had used me, and I have never recovered. It changed everything. I returned home and told Jane that I would leave the basketball world after my senior year and prepare to preach.

When we ended up in Wilmore, Kentucky, in the summer of 1969 as a newly married couple, God's providence once again proved uncanny. I was very interested in ideas, words, concepts, and literature of all kinds, but I had gotten through school without mastering the basics of grammar, syntax, spelling, and pronunciation. Apart from that, I was a genius. Jane was a master of all of these things; she even speaks other languages without an accent. She taught me to spell, write, and speak—you name it, she has been my teacher. When I was attempting to write my first book, she told me to relax and let it fly. Then she sat down and rewrote it. Those were the days of typewriters, when getting something right was a lot of work. In our house, it is still not unusual for me to yell to Jane, "How do you spell *hamstir*?" and for her to reply, "H-a-m-s-t-e-r."

The story continues; the beat goes on. As the years have gone by, we have pastored churches, raised sons, and loved their wives and sons together. We have traveled to over fifty countries in the world and have witnessed the great goodness and power of God in so many ways. God called me to be a writer, and there is no way I could have done it without the beautiful girl from the float. In fact, I have not done it—we have done it. You wouldn't be reading this book without God causing all things to work together for good. It is because of our union that my writing and study took the trajectory it has, that I have met and been influenced by the people I have: Dallas Willard, Eugene Peterson, and many more. I met Dallas Willard in 2001. Much of this book is a tribute to him and to his views on the gospel, especially the one that the gospel you believe in determines the disciple you make. That is why you are reading this book.

WHO MADE THE DECISIONS?

Who made the decisions that changed my life? Jane decided to date me, to forgive me, to attend ORU, to forgive me again, and to marry me. Were those decisions predetermined—did she really have a choice? When I saw her on the float, I wasn't a follower of Jesus, but my grandmother back in Indiana was praying for me; she had prayed for me every day of my life. When I knelt beside her on visits to her house, my six-foot-seven-inch frame next to her five-foot-zero-inch frame, she prayed for my salvation, for me to follow Jesus and to serve him. In Proverbs 16:1, it says, "We can make our own plans, but the LORD gives the right answer" (NLT). And 16:9 says: "We can make our plans, but the LORD determines our steps" (NLT). A life run by logic and reason alone is an either/or world. But we don't live in an either/or world—we live in a both/and world. Is it possible for God to work all things together for good and at the same time not violate your free will? The answer is that somehow, it seems that he does.

This book—like the speaker we started the chapter with—is asking you to make a change. The speaker asked you to do something about the millions going to hell without having heard the gospel. We have concluded that the responsibility the speaker was attempting to put on you was too heavy, a burden God never intended for you to carry. If you think making a bad decision or failing in some duty has the same effect as accidentally stepping on a mouse, you will be paralyzed with fear of doing the wrong thing or plagued by guilt for doing nothing.

So, what do you do? Stop thinking like a human. Bow your knee to a God who completely loves you and whose hand is on you. And drink these words in. Relax and allow them to serve you in this moment of decision:

> For God knew his people in advance, and he chose
> them to become like his Son, so that his Son would be
> the firstborn among many brothers and sisters. And
> having chosen them, he called them to come to him.
> And having called them, he gave them right standing
> with himself. And having given them right standing, he
> gave them his glory.
> What shall we say about such wonderful things
> as these? If God is for us, who can ever be against us?

Since he did not spare even his own Son but gave him up for us all, won't he also give us everything else? Who dares accuse us whom God has chosen for his own? No one—for God himself has given us right standing with himself. Who then will condemn us? No one—for Christ Jesus died for us and was raised to life for us, and he is sitting in the place of honor at God's right hand, pleading for us.

Can anything ever separate us from Christ's love? Does it mean he no longer loves us if we have trouble or calamity, or are persecuted, or hungry, or destitute, or in danger, or threatened with death? (As the Scriptures say, "For your sake we are killed every day; we are being slaughtered like sheep.") No, despite all these things, overwhelming victory is ours through Christ, who loved us.

And I am convinced that nothing can ever separate us from God's love. Neither death nor life, neither angels nor demons, neither our fears for today nor our worries about tomorrow—not even the powers of hell can separate us from God's love. No power in the sky above or in the earth below—indeed, nothing in all creation will ever be able to separate us from the love of God that is revealed in Christ Jesus our Lord.

ROMANS 8:29-39, NLT

We have presented you with the option to make your life's purpose to follow Jesus as his disciple and do what he did. This includes being part of his mission, the great commission. It means being a witness and participating in the larger call to make disciples of all nations as a member of his church. You might or might not have already been on board with Christ's plan for you. These wonderful words of Romans 8:29-39 tell a story of a God and his people: He knows you, loves you, and is fully committed to you. No one can bring accusations against you; God defends you and does not condemn you. If anyone condemns you, you have a defense in Christ himself. The passage even says that angels, demons, and your own fears and anxieties can't stop God from loving you and working with you. These are all true thoughts too wonderful for us to drink in completely. But we don't live in an either/or world—we live in a both/and world. Either/or theology says, "I'm good to go—leave me alone. God has my back. I'm free to sort this out on my own. I've got this."

Both/and thinking is evident as Paul continues in Romans chapter 10, especially as he reaches a conclusion:

> "Everyone who calls on the name of the LORD will be saved."
>
> But how can they call on him to save them unless they believe in him? And how can they believe in him if they have never heard about him? And how can they hear about him unless someone tells them? And how will anyone go and tell them without being sent?
>
> ROMANS 10:13-15, NLT

You are not just drifting about in the world—you were sent into the world. You are called to be conformed to the image of his Son, and what does his Son do? He was sent; therefore, you are sent. He served; therefore, you serve. He sacrificed; therefore, you sacrifice. That is the both/and life. Because salvation is indeed by discipleship alone. You can't really experience your salvation in an either/or posture; it is in a both/and world that you find your greatest joy. You will never fully understand all that is going on around you and inside of you. So, just like Brandon and me, stand up and start walking. Start following Jesus. Take all your doubts, questions, fears, and problems, and follow him. He will teach you everything you will ever need to know. And we shall see you along the path of obedience.

PAGES

It is clear by now there will be no great work, no magnum opus
No statue looking down serenely on crowds grateful for what I gave
No volume held with awe-struck hands by someone who,
Having poured over the pages, felt saved

But my God, my world is just so bright around me
The sun burning on my daughter's face, as she faces, with no hint
    of guilt nor guile, the coming day
As my son smiles and embraces, with quiet pleasure, the first
    orange light

I want to tell them
Be fruitful and multiply, fill the earth, flourish it
Pass down unwritten pages of life and love
And that tree will stand in the coming city with its many gardens
Where there are no statues, just oaks so full of sap they
    almost droop,
And seeds, flowering
As bees surround and crown
Their many leaves

ACKNOWLEDGMENTS

BILL: I would like to thank the National Leadership Team of the Bonhoeffer Project for their encouragement and partnership in changing leaders' minds, hearts, and habits. I would like to thank Brandon Cook for providing for me, an elder boomer, a window on the new world through which I can see.

BRANDON: And I would like to thank the community of Long Beach Christian Fellowship, and especially our board of elders, for their care, generosity, and tremendous support; my wife, Rebecca, for so often leaving me speechless; and Bill Hull, for illuminating so much of who I want to become on the path ahead.

INDEX OF POEMS

UNLESS OTHERWISE NOTED, each of the poems in *The Cost of Cheap Grace* was written by Brandon Cook. He posts these and other poems regularly at his website, www.storyflight.com, along with essays, stories, and prayers. Direct links for each of the poems in this book are found below.

NOTES

INTRODUCTION

1. *English Oxford Living Dictionaries*, s.v. "cliché (*n.*)," accessed April 24, 2019, https://en.oxforddictionaries.com/definition/cliche.
2. Dietrich Bonhoeffer, *Discipleship* (Minneapolis: Fortress, 2015), 4, 3.
3. Jordan B. Peterson, *Maps of Meaning: The Architecture of Belief* (New York: Routledge, 1999), 460.
4. Fyodor Dostoyevsky, *The Brothers Karamazov* (New York: Penguin, 2003), book V, chap. 4.
5. Dostoyevsky, *Brothers Karamazov*, book V, chap. 5.
6. Bill makes a similar point in *Conversion and Discipleship: You Can't Have One without the Other* (Grand Rapids, MI: Zondervan, 2016), chap. 1: "[The gospel] calls us to become apprentices of Christ and learn from him how to live our life as though he were living it."
7. Dietrich Bonhoeffer, *Dietrich Bonhoeffer Works, Vol. 4: Discipleship* (Minneapolis: Fortress, 2003), 49–50.
8. Walter Kaufmann, *Nietzsche: Philosopher, Psychologist, Antichrist* (Princeton, NJ: Princeton University Press, 2013), 343.
9. Please see Bill Hull's work in *Conversion and Discipleship*, 71–99.
10. Eugene H. Peterson, *Reversed Thunder: The Revelation of John and the Praying Imagination* (San Francisco: Harper & Row, 1988), 152.
11. Peterson, *Reversed Thunder*, 153.
12. Lesslie Newbigin, "Nihilism," lecture, audio recording, July 28, 2012, https://www.youtube.com/watch?v=5WyrC7JVd5Q.
13. Initially, Dallas Willard told me this story over lunch. Subsequently, I read it in one of the books put together after his death: *Eternal Living: Reflections on Dallas Willard's Teaching on Faith and Formation*, ed. by Gary W. Moon (Downers Grove, IL: IVP, 2015), 101.
14. Eugene Peterson, *Practice Resurrection: A Conversation on Growing Up in Christ* (Grand Rapids, MI: Eerdmans, 2010), 14.

15. Dietrich Bonhoeffer, *The Cost of Discipleship* (New York: Touchstone, 1995), 51.

1: THE DISCIPLE SHORTAGE

1. Brian Davies, *The Thought of Thomas Aquinas* (Oxford: Clarendon, 1993), 267.
2. Charles Malik, *The Two Tasks* (Westchester, IL: Billy Graham Center, 2000), 42.
3. Spurgeon used this analogy multiple times. In a sermon preached on June 10, 1886, he said it this way: "A great many learned men are defending the gospel; no doubt it is a very proper and right thing to do, yet I always notice that, when there are most books of that kind, it is because the gospel itself is not being preached. Suppose a number of persons were to take it into their heads that they had to defend a lion, a full-grown king of beasts! There he is in the cage, and here come all the soldiers of the army to fight for him. Well, I should suggest to them, if they would not object, and feel that it was humbling to them, that they should kindly stand back, and open the door, and let the lion out! I believe that would be the best way of defending him, for he would take care of himself; and the best 'apology' for the gospel is to let the gospel out." Elliot Ritzema, "Spurgeon's 'Let the lion out of the cage' quote," *All Is Grist* (blog), July 31, 2012, https://elliotritzema.com/2012 /07/31/spurgeons-let-the-lion-out-of-the-cage-quote/.
4. Dallas Willard, "State of Discipleship in the Church Today," *Renovating the Heart: Forming the Christ in Me Identity* (Christ Church of Oak Brook, Oak Brook, IL, November 4, 2005), MP3.
5. Lesslie Newbigin, *The Gospel in a Pluralist Society* (Grand Rapids, MI: Eerdmans, 1989), 240.
6. That other book is Bill Hull, *The Christian Leader: Rehabilitating Our Addiction to Secular Leadership* (Grand Rapids, MI: Zondervan, 2016).
7. Dietrich Bonhoeffer, *The Cost of Discipleship* (New York: Touchstone, 1995), 89.
8. James K. A. Smith, *You Are What You Love: The Spiritual Power of Habit* (Grand Rapids, MI: Brazos Press, 2016), 34–35.
9. Blue Letter Bible, s.v. "Lexicon: Strong's G3341 – *metanoia*," accessed June 10, 2019, https://www.blueletterbible.org/lang/lexicon/lexicon.cfm?t=kjv &strongs=g3341.
10. As quoted in Dave Earley and Rod Dempsey, *Disciple Making Is . . . How to Live the Great Commission with Passion and Confidence* (Nashville; B&H Academic, 2013), 91.

2: THE UPSIDE-DOWN KINGDOM

1. JR Woodward shared this idea with me in a private conversation. For more on it, see his *Creating a Missional Culture: Equipping the Church for the Sake of the World* (Downers Grove, IL: IVP, 2012), 32.

2. Plato, *Five Dialogues: Euthyphro, Apology, Crito, Meno, Phaedo*, 2nd ed. (Indianapolis, IN: Hackett, 2002), 41.

3. Plato writes in *The Republic*: "In the world of knowledge the idea of good appears last of all, and is seen . . . to be the universal author of all things beautiful and right" (Perth, Australia: Compass Circle, 2019), 233.

4. Bible Hub, s.v. "1343. *dikaiosuné*," accessed June 5, 2019, https://biblehub .com/greek/1343.htm.

5. Plato tasked philosophy with "delivering the soul from its bodily prison"; *Plato's Phaedo*, trans. R. Hackforth (Cambridge, UK: Cambridge University Press, 2001), chap. XI. This excerpt doesn't reflect Plato's complete stance on the body, however: See https://philosophynow.org/issues/122/Rediscovering _Platos_Vision. Nevertheless, this dualism—this separation of the body from the soul—was picked up and reinforced in later centuries, largely through the Neoplatonists and Gnostics.

6. Indeed, in Judaism, you get the notion of *tikkun olam*, the idea that we partner with God to see the world repaired and restored. For more on this concept, see Stan Meyer, "Tikkun Olam: Repairing the World," Jews for Jesus, accessed June 5, 2019, https://jewsforjesus.org/publications/issues /issues-v20-n03/tikkun-olam-repairing-the-world/.

7. Matthew W. Bates, *Salvation by Allegiance Alone: Rethinking Faith, Works, and the Gospel of Jesus the King* (Grand Rapids, MI: Baker Academic, 2017), 9.

8. Philosophy Terms, s.v. "*eudaimonia*," accessed June 5, 2019, https:// philosophyterms.com/eudaimonia/.

9. Perhaps the clearest modern iteration of this idea is found in Abraham Maslow's early theories of self-actualization.

10. Aristotle, *Nicomachean Ethics* (Oxford: Oxford University Press, 2009), Book I, chap. 7.16.

11. Aristotle, *Nicomachean Ethics*, Book II, chap. 6.5.

12. The conclusion Weinandy ultimately draws in his survey of classic and modern arguments for and against a passible God—a God who truly suffers—is for the impassibility of God, which has been the dominant position within Christian thought and remains so despite the rise of process theology. See his "Conclusion" in Thomas G. Weinandy, *Does God Suffer?* (Notre Dame, IN: University of Notre Dame Press, 2000).

13. Jonathan Sacks, "The Story We Tell (Ki Tavo 5778)," *Office of Rabbi Sacks* (podcast), August 28, 2018, http://rabbisacks.org/story-tell-ki-tavo-5778/.

14. Luc Ferry argues that this personal notion of salvation within Christian thought is what allowed Christianity to triumph over Greek philosophy. See *A Brief History of Thought: A Philosophical Guide to Living* (New York: Harper Perennial, 2011), chap. 3.

15. Dallas Willard, "The Good Person: A Matter of the Heart," unpublished manuscript presented at a Christian counselors' conference in 2007, accessed April 29, 2019, http://www.dwillard.org/articles/individual/good-person-a -matter-of-the-heart-the.

16. John, for example, takes the Greek word *Logos*, a central idea in Stoic thought, then subverts its meaning. The entirely transcendent *Logos* becomes, literally, entirely immanent; the *Logos* becomes enfleshed and embodied.

17. Dallas Willard, *The Divine Conspiracy: Rediscovering Our Hidden Life in God* (New York: HarperSanFrancisco, 1998), chap. 7.

18. *Merriam-Webster*, s.v. "summum bonum (*n.*)," accessed April 30, 2019, http://unabridged.merriam-webster.com/unabridged/summum+bonum.

19. *Merriam-Webster*, s.v. "paterfamilias (*n.*)," accessed April 30, 2019, http://unabridged.merriam-webster.com/unabridged/paterfamilias.

20. See René Girard's mimetic theory in *I See Satan Fall Like Lightning* (Maryknoll, NY: Orbis Books, 2001), chap. 11: "The Triumph of the Cross."

21. Rabbi Lord Sacks, "Why the World Needs Rosh Hashanah," *Jewish Chronicle*, September 7, 2018, https://www.thejc.com/comment/comment/why-the-world-needs-rosh-hashanah-jonathan-lord-sacks-1.469442.

22. "Episode 8: Jonathan Haidt," interview by Jonathan Sacks, September 3, 2018, in *Morality in the 21st Century*, produced by Dan Tierney, BBC Radio 4, podcast, 31:53, https://www.bbc.co.uk/programmes/p06k4sx8.

23. Leonardo Blair, "Tim Keller Warns Christians about Being Divided by Politics: 'You're Christian First,'" *Christian Post*, October 28, 2016, https://www.christianpost.com/news/tim-keller-warns-christians-about-being-divided-by-politics-youre-christian-first.html.

24. Michael Love Michael, "Celebrities Are Identifying as Pansexual, Here's What That Means" *Paper*, April 27, 2018, http://www.papermag.com/celebrities-pansexual-2563888076.html.

25. Noted in a personal conversation.

26. As Charles Taylor notes in *Sources of the Self: The Making of Modern Identity* (Cambridge, MA: Harvard University, 1992), part I, human dignity is well and good as a value, but if it's the only value, it's insufficient to form a moral horizon.

27. Warren Cole Smith, "Inexpressive: Hesed and the Mystery of God's Loving Kindness," February 18, 2019, in *Breakpoint* podcast, http://www.breakpoint.org/2019/02/inexpressible-hesed-and-the-mystery-of-gods-loving-kindness/.

28. Willard, *Divine Conspiracy*, 2: "This is a parable of human existence in our times—not exactly that everyone is crashing, though there is enough of that—but most of us as individuals, and world society as a whole, live at high-speed, and often with no clue as to whether we are flying upside down or right-side up. Indeed, we are haunted by a strong suspicion that there may be no difference—or at least that it is unknown or irrelevant."

3: THE GOSPEL AMERICANA

1. See my explanation of the history of the gospel being replaced by the plan of salvation in *Conversion and Discipleship* (Grand Rapids, MI: Zondervan, 2016), 28–32.

2. Hull, *Conversion and Discipleship*, 23–47.
3. Dallas Willard, in a letter to Bill Hull. Cited from Hull, *Conversion and Discipleship*, 206.
4. See *The Gay Science* (sections 108, 125, 343) and *Thus Spoke Zarathustra* (prologue, XXV).
5. Fyodor Dostoyevsky, *The Brothers Karamazov* (New York: Penguin, 2003), book V, chap. 5.
6. Bob Smietana, "Prosperity Gospel Taught to 4 in 10 Evangelical Churchgoers," *Christianity Today*, July 31, 2018. LifeWay Research conducted the survey.
7. David W. Jones, "Five Errors of the Prosperity Gospel," Gospel Coalition, June 5, 2015, https://www.thegospelcoalition.org/article/5-errors-of-the -prosperity-gospel/. This statement by Dollar is built around Mark 11:23-25. The passage could be construed to mean what he proposes it means, but he removed the context and some of the conditions, then claimed that God was contractually obligated to answer such a prayer. It puts the person praying in charge, limited only by his or her own faith; according to this line of thinking, God becomes helpless to make his own decision.
8. This is the average. (See David P. King and Thad Austin, "Religious Giving Holds Steady: First Reflections on Giving USA 2017," Lilly Family School of Philanthropy, June 13, 2017, https://philanthropy.iupui.edu/news-events /insights-newsletter/2017-issues/june-2017-issue1.html.) Four facts that relate to this are: (1) tithers make up only 10 to 25 percent of any congregation; (2) eight out of ten people who give to churches have zero credit-card debt; (3) religious giving is down about 50 percent since 1990; and (4) on average, Christians give 2.5 percent of their income to churches. (Jayson D. Bradley, "Church Giving Statistics, 2018 Edition," July 18, 2018, https://pushpay.com/blog/church-giving-statistics/.)
9. Pew Research Center, "Attendance at Religious Services," 2014 U.S. Religious Landscape Study, accessed May 2, 2019, http://www.pewforum .org/religious-landscape-study/attendance-at-religious-services/.
10. Barna, "Is Evangelism Going Out of Style?," December 17, 2013, https:// www.barna.com/research/is-evangelism-going-out-of-style/.
11. Notes taken on retreat, June 8–19, 2009, Sierra Madre, CA, on a talk from Dallas Willard.
12. For example, in a sermon entitled "Free Grace," he said: "I abhor the doctrine of predestination; a doctrine, upon the supposition of which, if one could possibly suppose it for a moment . . . one might say to our adversary the devil, 'Thou fool, why dost thou roar about any longer? Thy lying in wait for souls is as needless and useless as our preaching. Hearest thou not, that God hath taken thy work out of thy hands; and that he doeth it much more effectively?'"; *The Works of the Rev. John Wesley*, vol. I (New York: Carlton & Phillips, 1853), 489.
13. See Arnold A. Dallimore, *George Whitefield: The Life and Times of the Great*

Evangelist of the 18th-Century Revival (Carlisle, PA: Banner of Truth Trust, 1980).

14. Barna Group, "New Barna Global Study Examines the UK Church," May 29, 2018, https://www.barna.com/research/what-the-uk-doesnt-know-about-the -church/.

15. Barna Group, "51% of Churchgoers Don't Know of the Great Commission," March 27, 2018, https://www.barna.com/research/half-churchgoers-not -heard-great-commission/.

4: A NATION OF HERETICS

1. Online Etymology Dictionary, s.v. "heresy (*n.*)," accessed May 3, 2019, https://www.etymonline.com/word/heresy.

2. Some people claim that Darwin waited so long to publish *Origin* because of his involvement in other time-consuming projects. See, for example, "Darwin's Delay the Stuff of Myth," University of Cambridge: Research, accessed June 11, 2019, https://www.cam.ac.uk/research/news/%C2%93darwins-delay %C2%94-the-stuff-of-myth. But others attribute Darwin's delay to "fear of a backlash from Britain's religious and even scientific establishment" ("Darwin and His Theory of Evolution," Pew Research Center, February 4, 2009, https://www.pewforum.org/2009/02/04/darwin-and-his-theory-of-evolution/).

3. Online Etymology Dictionary, s.v. "nihilism (*n.*)," accessed May 3, 2019, https://www.etymonline.com/word/nihilism.

4. Nietzsche didn't coin this term, but he used it heavily (forty-seven times) in *Also Sprach Zarathustra*; see Encyclopaedia Britannica, s.v. "Superman," accessed June 5, 2019, https://www.britannica.com/topic/superman-philosophy.

5. The points being made are a compilation taken from three sources. First is Lesslie Newbigin's book *Foolishness to the Greeks* (Grand Rapids, MI: Eerdmans, 1988). The second is a message given by Newbigin on nihilism (https://www.youtube.com/watch?v=5WyrC7JVd5Q). Third is Tim Keller's speech, "'Answering Lesslie Newbigin,' Tim Keller's 2017 Kuyper Lecture" at Princeton Seminary on April 6, 2017 (https://www.youtube.com/watch ?v=V0LG26k6ngs).

6. Based on a study of Scotland, Ireland, and the UK; Barna Global, *The UK Church in Action: Perceptions of Social Justice and Mission in a Changing World* (London: Barna Global, 2018).

7. James W. Sire, *The Universe Next Door: A Basic Worldview Catalog*, 5th ed. (Downers Grove, IL: IVP Academic, 2009).

8. This point is not from a specific Pearcey book; rather, it's a simple formula I've gleaned from a variety of sources.

9. Nancy Pearcey, *Total Truth: Liberating Christianity from Its Cultural Captivity* (Wheaton, IL: Crossway, 2004), 25.

10. See, for example, https://www.culturalsurvival.org/publications/cultural -survival-quarterly/survival-tibetan-culture and https://www.khanacademy

.org/humanities/world-history/ancient-medieval/early-indian-empires/a
/hinduism-in-indian-culture.

11. As quoted in Adam L. Gustine, *Becoming a Just Church: Cultivating Communities of God's Shalom* (Downers Grove, IL; IVP, 2019), 66.

12. I have chosen three out of the seven conditions Newbigin presents as necessary for a missionary encounter with our culture in *Foolishness to the Greeks*, 134–150.

13. Tim Keller, "A World of Idols," January 12, 2018, audio, https://www .youtube.com/watch?v=KLVxQh5qggY.

14. This is based on it being an imperfect tense and the passive voice. The imperfect tense means that something in the past made Paul angry and the results continue. The passive voice means that the reason for the provocation came from outside the person (Paul, in this case). See Fritz Rienecker and Cleon L. Rogers, *A Linguistic Key to the Greek New Testament* (Grand Rapids, MI: Zondervan, 1976), 307.

15. Keller, "A World of Idols."

16. Ibid.

17. Richard Pallardy, "12 Greek Gods and Goddesses," *Encyclopaedia Britannica*, accessed May 7, 2019, https://www.britannica.com/list/12-greek-gods-and -goddesses.

18. Lesslie Newbigin, "Nihilism," lecture, audio recording, July 28, 2012, https://www.youtube.com/watch?v=5WyrC7JVd5Q.

19. Lesslie Newbigin, "Can the West Be Converted?," *International Bulletin of Missionary Research* 11, no. 1 (January 1987): 2, http://www .internationalbulletin.org/issues/1987-01/1987-01-002-newbigin.pdf. His discussion of Berger's ideas addresses Peter L. Berger, *The Heretical Imperative: Contemporary Possibilities of Religious Affirmation* (Garden City, NY: Anchor, 1979).

20. Eric Metaxas, *Seven Women and the Secret of Their Greatness* (Nashville: Nelson Books, 2015), 176.

21. Newbigin, "Nihilism," lecture.

5: RETURNING TO THE BIBLICAL GOSPEL

1. "For it is impossible for a man to begin to learn that which he thinks that he knows." *The Discourses of Epictetus: With the Encheiridion and Fragments*, trans. George Long (London: George Bell and Sons, 1877), Book II, chap. 17.

2. Matthew W. Bates, *Salvation by Allegiance Alone* (Grand Rapids, MI: Baker Academic, 2017), 15. Emphasis in original.

3. Paul, after all, called himself a "bondservant" of Christ Jesus (e.g., Romans 1:1, NKJV).

4. In this way, Jesus' invitation to be transformed by grace is the constant answer to our desire to be better people. Mere "trying harder" is subverted by becoming open to grace; we reframe the question "How can I be/become good enough?"

to "God, how can you be so good as to receive me when I *was* not/*am* not good enough?"; and we escape the either/or thinking that we are good or not good based on the strength of our willpower and enter into the both/and realization that our willpower is needed, but it's God's grace that transforms us.

5. See Bates's *Salvation by Allegiance Alone*, pages 107–110. It is not the aim of this volume to delve into the theology underlying the confusion between allegiance-based salvation and the biblical, New Testament demand for transformation as a natural part of salvation; suffice it to say that this is not the biblical view, at least as it was understood in the first century.

6. John Barclay demonstrates that in antiquity, a gift received always demanded a response. There was little cultural notion of "a free gift," such as we value today. See *Paul and the Gift* by John M. G. Barclay (Grand Rapids, MI: Eerdmans, 2017), 24–65.

7. Edwin Friedman describes as "stuck" any system caught in false dichotomies and poor thinking; *A Failure of Nerve: Leadership in the Age of the Quick Fix* (New York: Church Publishing, 1999). The argument here is that the American church has been stuck in either/or thinking and that this thinking is not only a sign but also a symptom of the Gospel Americana. See Friedman's analysis in chapter 1, "Imaginative Gridlock and the Spirit of Adventure."

8. Adrian Pei, *The Minority Experience: Navigating Emotional and Organizational Realities* (Downers Grove, IL: IVP, 2018), 65.

9. The focus on external action without internal transformation is at the heart of Jesus' critique of the religion of the Pharisees. For example, see Matthew 23.

10. See Marvin R. Wilson, *Our Father Abraham: Jewish Roots of the Christian Faith* (Grand Rapids, MI: Eerdmans, 1989), especially chap. 9.

11. The frustration of Western philosophy has been trying to resolve two very different worldviews, Greek and Hebrew. In Greek thought, God is the Unmoved Mover, perfectly dispassionate. In Hebrew thought, he is the Most Moved Mover, full of pathos. How does one resolve such different conceptions of the divine? The failure of Western philosophy is the failure to bridge these metaphysical ideas, which requires both/and thinking. Ironically, our recent scientific discoveries of the physical universe have pointed us out of dualistic thinking and into both/and. Quantum mechanics tells, for example, that light is somehow both a wave and a particle, leaving those committed to either/or thinking frustrated, even in the presence of the light itself.

12. It's a question apparently born out of the Deuteronomic tradition, with its focus on "do good and good will come to you; do bad and bad will come to you." There is truth in this way of thinking; we all know that. But it's not the whole truth, as later biblical books like Ecclesiastes and Job sought to address: Bad things *do* happen to good people, and what do we do with that?

13. Skye Jethani, *With: Reimagining the Way You Relate to God* (Nashville: Thomas Nelson, 2011), 9, 63.

14. Notice how slippery language is and how one word can mean different

things: Even the word *church* refers to the people of God from every tribe and tongue, whereas *the local church* means something much narrower.

15. See page 9.
16. Wendell Berry, "Christianity and the Survival of Creation," *CrossCurrents* 43, no. 2 (Summer 1993), http://www.crosscurrents.org/berry.htm.
17. Much of Wright's work illuminates this scriptural theme. See, for example, *Surprised by Hope: Rethinking Heaven, the Resurrection, and the Mission of the Church* (New York: HarperOne, 2008), 104–108.
18. See, for instance, Matthew 19:29; 25:46; John 4:36; 5:24; 6:40; 10:28; 12:25; 12:50.
19. C. S. Lewis, *The Last Battle* (New York: HarperCollins, 2005), chap. 15.
20. Gregory Boyd calls the supposed transformation of our souls at death despite no purification of them on earth "zap doctrine." Greg Boyd, "Between Here and Heaven: What Are Your Views on Purgatory?" in *Apologies and Explanations*, podcast, 9:43, June 1, 2018, https://askgregboyd.libsyn.com /between-here-and-heaven-what-are-your-views-on-purgatory.
21. From personal correspondence with Bill.
22. As Willard also wrote, "The fires of heaven burn hotter than the fires of hell"; Dallas Willard, *The Allure of Gentleness: Defending the Faith in the Manner of Jesus* (New York: HarperOne, 2015), 67.
23. Scot McKnight, foreword to Bates, *Salvation by Allegiance Alone.*
24. See Galatians 2:16 and the debate of the translation of *pistis christou.* We favor, following N. T. Wright and Matthew Bates, among others, the translation "faithfulness of Christ." See, for example: Trevin Wax, "'Faith IN Christ' or 'Faithfulness OF Christ,'" The Gospel Coalition, May 23, 2011, https://www.thegospelcoalition.org/blogs/trevin-wax/faith-in-christ-or -faithfulness-of-christ/.
25. In a personal conversation with Bill.
26. Dallas Willard, "How Does the Disciple Live?," originally delivered as a talk, for which the text is now available online: http://www.dwillard.org/articles /individual/how-does-the-disciple-live. See also Dallas Willard, *The Great Omission: Reclaiming Jesus' Essential Teachings on Discipleship* (New York: HarperOne, 2006), 114.
27. This was noted in a personal conversation with Ben, but for more on the dimensions of grace in Scripture, see Bill Hull and Ben Sobels, *The Discipleship Gospel: What Jesus Preached—We Must Follow* (Brentwood, TN: HIM, 2018). This argument is elucidated over the course of the book, as Sobels unpacks grace in the context of the early disciples' experience.
28. Paul, for example, says that grace was given him to be a minister (1 Corinthians 15:9-10).
29. Bible Hub, s.v. "7725. *shub*," accessed June 6, 2019, https://biblehub.com /hebrew/7725.htm.

30. Bible Hub, s.v. "3341. *metanoia*," accessed June 6, 2019, https://biblehub
.com/greek/3341.htm.
31. Rikk Watts, "Creation as God's Temple," in "It's about Life: A Biblical
Journey," Regent Audio, March 18, 2011, 5:31:00, https://www.regentaudio
.com/products/its-about-life-a-biblical-journey. Also see Leslie Hilburn,
"Holy of Holies and Ark of the Covenant," Christian Churches of God,
http://www.ccg.org/weblibs/children-papers/cb112.html.
32. The notion that God always provides a way out (1 Corinthians 10:13) is
quite different from the notion that God is stacking on our shoulders as
much as we can handle.
33. Speaking of metaphors, I heard this wonderful starting-line/finish-line
metaphor from Keith Foster, a faculty member in The Bonhoeffer Project.
34. Justification (*dikaiōsis*) was used in contemporary Greek society to describe
the acquittal of prisoners. But in the broader Hebraic sense (*tsadeq*), it
connoted being brought in right relationship with God and was generally
linked to the Hebrew word *mishpat*, associated with doing justice in the
world—that is, being in right relationship with others. We have a say in
whether we interpret justification through its individual transactional reality
or its broader, interrelational reality. Salvation includes both.

6: RUNNING WITH HORSES

1. Barna Group, "The State of the Church 2016," September 15, 2016, https://
www.barna.com/research/state-church-2016/.
2. Robert Webber and Lester Ruth, *Evangelicals on the Canterbury Trail: Why
Evangelicals Are Attracted to the Liturgical Church* (New York: Morehouse,
2013).
3. For example, Ian Morgan Cron and Suzanne Stabile, *The Road Back to You: An
Enneagram Journey to Self-Discovery* (Downers Grove, IL: IVP Books, 2016).
4. Part of Renovaré's "six stream" description. See Renovaré, "The Six Streams:
A Balanced Vision," accessed May 10, 2019, https://renovare.org/about
/ideas/the-six-streams, and Richard J. Foster, *Streams of Living Water:
Essential Practices from the Six Great Traditions of Christian Faith* (New York:
HarperSanFrancisco, 2001), chap. 6.
5. René Descartes, *Discourse on Method and Meditations on First Philosophy*, 4th
ed. (Indianapolis, IN: Hackett, 1998), part IV.32.
6. Remarked in a private conversation with Bill.
7. Quoted in Charles Marsh, *Strange Glory: A Life of Dietrich Bonhoeffer* (New
York: Knopf, 2014), 384.
8. Commentary by Bryan Rouanzoin in personal conversation.
9. For example, the older brother in the parable of the two sons (Luke 15:11-32).
10. Quoted in Ashley Hamilton, "What's the Key to a Meaningful Life? You
Might Not Like the Answer," *Huffington Post*, March 15, 2016, https://
www.huffingtonpost.com/entry/david-brooks-life-meaning_us
_56e6f962e4b0b25c9182b0c3.

11. M. Robert Mulholland, *Invitation to a Journey: A Road Map for Spiritual Formation* (Downers Grove, IL: IVP Books, 1993), 87–93. The false self is what Paul describes in Romans 8 as the sinful nature—"the flesh"—which is the part of us that does not want to be dependent on God; in modern parlance, we would call it the "ego."

12. Bible Hub, s.v. "4383. *prosópon*," accessed June 6, 2019, https://biblehub.com/greek/4383.htm.

13. Thank you to my friend Darren Adwalpalker for illuminating this passage for me.

14. See Bill Hull, *Conversion and Discipleship* (Grand Rapids, MI: Zondervan, 2016), chaps. 4 and 5.

15. Quoted in "Iona Liturgy Homily" by Richard Rohr in *Homilies*, podcast, July 28, 2018, https://cac.org/podcasts/conspire-2018-iona-liturgy-homily/.

16. Catherine McNiel, *Long Days of Small Things: Motherhood as a Spiritual Discipline* (Colorado Springs, CO: NavPress, 2017).

17. Henri Nouwen, "From Solitude to Community to Ministry," *Christianity Today*, April 1, 1995, https://www.christianitytoday.com/pastors/1995/spring/5l280.html.

18. Mike Breen, *Building a Discipling Culture: How to Release a Missional Movement by Discipling People Like Jesus Did* (Greenville, SC: 3DM, 2017), chap. 7.

19. Discussed in Brandon Cook, *Learning to Live and Love Like Jesus: A Discipleship Journey for Groups and Individuals* (self-pub., 2018), chaps. 1–3.

20. Ibid., chaps. 7–18.

7: THE RIGHT DIRT

1. Nancy R. Pearcey, "Copying the Human Script: Genome Project Raises Hopes, Fears," *World*, July 8, 2000, http://libertyparkusafd.org/Paley/Journal/2000/Copying%20the%20Human%20Script%20-%20%20Genome%20Project%20Raises%20Hopes,%20Fears.htm.

2. This statement, made to Jesus' disciples, differentiated them from those who did not listen to his teaching.

3. I can't say that there are any direct quotes in this paragraph, but I did benefit from reading a Tim Keller sermon on this subject ("The Sower; On Hearing," 2017) and thank him for this idea about listening.

4. Upton Sinclair, *I, Candidate for Governor: And How I Got Licked* (Berkeley, CA: University of California Press, 1994), 109.

5. As cited in Preston Sprinkle, *Go: Returning Discipleship to the Front Lines of Faith* (Colorado Springs, CO: NavPress, 2016), 89.

6. Dallas Willard, *The Divine Conspiracy: Rediscovering Our Hidden Life in God* (New York: HarperSanFrancisco, 1998), 303.

7. See Biblical Training, "Tyrannus," accessed June 6, 2019, https://www.biblicaltraining.org/library/tyrannus.

8. The mission church, as I call it in *The Disciple-Making Church: Leading a Body of Believers on the Journey of Faith* (Grand Rapids, MI: Baker Books,

2010), 109–205, covers Paul's time in Ephesus and catalogs all the church leaders from the mission church that visited him the three years he resided in Ephesus.

9. Paul claims that through direct revelation Jesus taught him the gospel.

CONCLUSION: DECIDE

1. Geoffrey Wainwright, *Lesslie Newbigin: A Theological Life* (New York: Oxford University Press, 2000), 201.

2. Lesslie Newbigin, "Nihilism," lecture, audio recording, July 28, 2012, https://www.youtube.com/watch?v=5WyrC7JVd5Q.

3. Ibid.

4. Ibid.

5. *The Book of Common Prayer*, according to the use of The Episcopal Church (New York: Church Publishing Incorporated, 1979), 339.

6. Tim Keller, "Does God Control Everything?" audio recording, January 9, 2018, https://www.youtube.com/watch?v=zvzajsUU6sE.

7. Said at a panel at an Exponential conference (Mariners Church, Newport Beach, California, October 3, 2016).

8. J. I. Packer, *Evangelism and the Sovereignty of God* (Downers Grove, IL: IVP, 2012), 23–40.

9. Tim Keller, "Does God Control Everything?" audio recording, January 9, 2018, https://www.youtube.com/watch?v=zvzajsUU6sE. Transcript by rev.com, completed September 1, 2018, page 13.

10. Keller, "Does God Control Everything?" The referenced short story by Ray Bradbury is "A Sound of Thunder," accessed May 21, 2019, https://www.rosaryhs.com/s/1514/images/editor_documents/academics/2017-18/a-sound-of-thunder.pdf?no_cookie=1.

11. Keller, "Does God Control Everything?"

12. "Thus saith the Lord: 'Behold, I have lifted up mine hand to the Gentiles, and set up my standard to the people, and they shall bring thy sons in their arms and on their breasts: kings shall be thy nursing fathers and queens thy nursing mothers: they shall bow down to thee with their face towards the earth, *and lick up the dust of thy feet*; and thou shalt know that I am the Lord . . .,"; Blaise Pascal, *Pensées*, trans. by A. J. Krailsheimer (London: Penguin, 1995), 155. Emphasis added.

ABOUT THE AUTHORS

BILL HULL is a discipleship evangelist. He has spent his ministry life helping the church return to its disciple-making roots. Two of his more important books, *Jesus Christ, Disciplemaker* and *The Disciple-Making Pastor*, have both celebrated twenty years in print.

BRANDON COOK serves as pastor of vision and teaching at Long Beach Christian Fellowship. Originally from Birmingham, Alabama, Brandon studied at Wheaton College, Jerusalem University College, Brandeis University, and the Oxford Centre for Hebrew and Jewish Studies. Before moving to Southern California in 2006, he worked as a professional storyteller.

In 2014, Bill and Brandon cofounded the Bonhoeffer Project, a yearlong leadership development community designed to help Christians reclaim the discipleship-first gospel, craft a disciple-making plan, and make disciples who make disciples. More information is available at thebonhoefferproject.com.